TALKING WITH HORSES

A Study of Communication between Man and Horse

H. N. BLAKE

SOUVENIR PRESS

Contents

Foreword

This book is based on forty years' work with horses, the last twenty of which have been spent studying how they communicate, with each other and with man. My wife Leslie and my daughter Paddy have both taken a full part in this research – hence the frequent use of the pronoun 'we' in the text.

My motivation was simple – I wanted to achieve a greater understanding with my horses, and so to attain better performance on the racecourse and in competitions; and the way to such attainment I soon found to be through increasing the horses' own enjoyment of life. It was only towards the end of our research that we began to think our work might be of interest to other people. This book has been written in the hope that others will benefit from, and in due course build on, what we have learned.

H. N. Blake

1: *Horses I have Learned From*

Maybe I am not quite sane, but horses have been my whole life. For me they are a drug more potent than LSD and more lethal than heroin. My friends tell me that my addiction has already produced deterioration of the brain. And unlike any other drug, horses are a drug for which there is no known cure: for me life without horses would be only a living death.

My earliest memories are of horses rather than people, and horses rather than places or people have represented the milestones of my life. I am a true centaur, half man, half horse.

The first thing I remember is sitting on a horse in front of my great-uncle Harvey Blake: I must have been little more than a year old. And I remember that just after this my father bought a black thoroughbred gelding called Masterpiece, a horse that was extremely difficult to handle, for he used to kick and strike out with his front legs at anybody who came into his stable. I had not been walking for very long when a general panic was caused in the household, because I was missing and could not be found anywhere. After a considerable time my mother and father, nursemaid and the farmhands, all of whom were looking for me, found me in the stables coolly playing under Masterpiece's manger. When they tried to get me out, Masterpiece used his feet and teeth to prevent anybody passing the door. Eventually I had to be tempted out with a sweet from the doorway, after which I always used Masterpiece's stable as my favourite refuge, where I could play undisturbed with the horse protecting me. I used to wander about under his legs and feet and thoroughly enjoy myself, as a small boy will, getting myself filthy. Further, being rather an unpleasant child, I quickly found that when

9

I was naughty I could escape punishment there as long as I wanted, while my nursemaid and parents fumed outside the door. I used to refuse to come out until they promised not to spank me. This experience taught me at a very early age that horses were my friends and protectors.

In the autumn of 1933 my parents went to Bridgwater Fair and paid two pounds for a small black Dartmoor pony. Inevitably she was called Black Beauty and she became the guide, teacher and friend of the whole family. A great individualist, she could untie any rope and open any door. On one occasion when we were trying to corner her in the yard, she escaped by going through the back door of the pantry into the kitchen, out to the hall and then out through the front door. And when we were sick, she would be brought up the stairs to our bedrooms to keep us company as a reward for good behaviour. A very stern disciplinarian, she punished any bad practice in a rider by depositing him firmly on the ground, and then waiting to be remounted, teaching me very early in life that a horse will retaliate instantly against any infringement of its code of conduct.

When the time came for me to go to school the obvious way to get me there and back was on a pony, and when a year or two later my younger sister joined me, she used to ride behind. We always rode bareback, as my father was of the opinion that the only way to learn a true seat on a horse was to ride without a saddle. We learnt to trot, canter and even to jump long before we had a saddle, which we were allowed to have when we were seven.

And so for the next five or six years, until I went to boarding school, I rode to school every day. Occasionally, if we were very very lucky, we would go down in the morning to find that the ponies had got out of the field; and provided the weather was nice, that would be a 'red letter' day, spent looking for ponies and being damned careful not to find them.

The next horse who played a really significant part in my education was a New Forest thoroughbred-cross chestnut mare, who had been bred as a polo pony. Chester was very difficult to handle in the stable. Since she had a very thin skin and was very ticklish, she would kick and scream in temper if anyone touched her legs or tried to groom her. But she was the first horse with which I ever established a real understanding and empathy, and I found after a while I could anticipate what she was going to do before she did it, and that she in turn would reflect my moods. As a result she was a fantastic gymkhana pony and for two years I supplemented my pocket money with her winnings.

While I still had Chester, another horse arrived who was to teach me a great deal. One day the local knacker man, Bert Newman, who for years had sold my father horses he thought too good to kill, telephoned to say he had a bay sixteen-two-hand three-quarter-thoroughbred mare, four years old, and he would let my father have her very cheaply for ten pounds. My father said that there were too many damned horses about the place and he did not want another one, so Bert said he would let my father have her for a fiver. 'No thank you,' was the reply. The exchange ended with Bert saying that, because of their long-standing friendship, he was giving the mare to my father and would send her over at once. I was thirteen at this time and still riding to school. When I got home that evening, the mare had been unloaded from the lorry into a covered yard with some heifers, and I managed after some argument to persuade my father to let me ride her to school the next day.

The following morning I went out to the yard to catch her and bring her into the stable. But instead of eating from the proffered bowl of oats, she attacked me with her teeth and front legs, so I clouted her across the nose with a halter and told her not to be a bloody-minded cow. I put the halter on, saddled and bridled her and rode her off to school.

About five minutes past nine Bert telephoned. He had had a bad night nagged by a guilty conscience, he said, and my father was not to touch the mare as she was dangerous. When he heard that I had already ridden her to school, the full story came out. Fearless had killed her previous owner, a Devonshire farmer, and Bert had been paid to take her away. He had intended to shoot her as soon as she came off the lorry, but unfortunately an R.S.P.C.A. official had arrived and insisted that she be put down with a humane killer in his presence, and since this was clearly impossible Bert had thought of my father.

I rode Fearless to school for the next two weeks, and apart from the fact that she was inclined to take a piece out of me with her teeth and strike at me with her front legs, I had no trouble whatsoever. We kept her until she died and she repaid us a thousand times, as she saved me twice from serious injury and on one occasion saved my father's life.

My father was driving home with her and a young horse as a pair in a wagon, when the young horse bolted at an American Army convoy. Fearless steered the cart and the other horse in and out of the convoy and the oncoming traffic, and eventually managed to stop the other horse. This she did by swinging away and pulling the young horse with her when she wanted to go to the left, and when she wanted to go to the right by swinging her head and biting the young horse to make it shy away. My father could not do anything with the reins since the young horse had panicked and was completely uncontrollable, but Fearless could control him, and she managed eventually to stop him after about two miles.

Fearless was always bloody-minded, but there was no horse like her. My first encounter with her had taught me a lesson I have remembered ever since: that with horses, if you are without fear and confident of yourself, you will be able to master any situation.

Fearless was such a good worker we never chose to breed from her, but finally when she was eleven years old her frustration got the better of her, and one night she got out into the neighbouring field where we had a bunch of yearlings and two-year-olds running. Among them was an immature uncut two-year-old thoroughbred who was barely fourteen-two. Fearless was well over sixteen-two, and my father always swore that she went up into the yard and borrowed a step-ladder; but anyway, during the night she somehow managed to persuade the young Corsican – that was the two-year-old's name – to serve her, and eleven months later, full of pride and joy, she produced a son and celebrated the fact by taking a piece out of me when I went down to congratulate her. There was only one name that he could be called and that was Folly. He became the property of my sister Olive, and for the next five years he grew and thrived.

When he was three years old he was broken, and after breaking him I taught him to buck on command. I could always make him buck in a dead straight line, a very big and powerful buck that was nevertheless extremely easy to sit, so at the age of eighteen this was my standard party piece when I wanted to show off to my girl-friends. My father played polo on him and my sister Olive hunted him.

Eventually, just before she went out to New Guinea as a medical missionary, Olive decided she would like to fulfil an old ambition and ride in a point-to-point. Since she weighed twelve stone seven pounds and stood five feet ten inches, this was clearly a piece of madness. But when Olive makes up her mind to anything there is no arguing with her, so she entered Folly for the ladies' race at the Axe Vale point-to-point. For the whole of that season two horses had been dominating the ladies' races in the West Country – Ching Ling and Shepherd's Pie. So unbeatable were these two that everyone else eventually gave up, and when we got to the Axe Vale we discovered there was nothing else in the race : only Ching Ling, Shepherd's Pie and Folly.

Olive borrowed my breeches, racing colours and boots, and ate a hearty breakfast. Apart from instructing her that even if she broke her neck, she was to get back to the paddock to give me back my racing colours, there was not much else I could do to avert the coming disaster. She also insisted on riding in a hunting saddle, since she had never ridden in anything else.

Olive and Folly clearly decided that this was a first-class hunt and nothing more, so they proceeded for two-and-a-half miles at a steady speed. At last, half a mile from home, Olive decided that now was the time to do something about winning the race, and since Ching Ling and Shepherd's Pie were then a fence and a half in front of her, I thought she was leaving it a bit late! But Folly went; and it was only because he was giving two-and-a-half stone away to the two best ladies'-race horses in the West of England, that he was beaten by five lengths. What he would have done if he had started his run in good time, I clearly do not know. I am quite sure that the public, none of whom had backed Olive, would have lynched her if she had won, so it was probably just as well she took her time. But they both enjoyed themselves, and that little story only shows just what a good horse will do for its owner when he really puts his mind to it.

The following year Folly was sold to some friends of ours and he was still hunting and hunting well when we left the West Country ten years ago.

Shortly after the experience with Fearless, my father realized that in handling unmanageable horses he was on to a good thing. So he put a series of advertisements in the *Horse and Hound*: BAD'NS AND MAD'NS BOUGHT AND BROKEN.

For the next five or ten years a series of unbreakable and unrideable horses arrived at Martock and Crewkerne Stations, each of which was about four miles from my home. It being war time, and help being scarce, I was sent to fetch them, and was always given strict instructions to lead the horses home. But I was bone lazy as well as disobedient, and saw no reason why I should walk when there was a horse to ride, so apart from the first and last half mile, I used to ride them home in a halter. I got plenty of secret amusement out of the next day, when my father went through the full breaking procedure before considering the horse safe for me to mount. I realized of course that the reason I found these unrideable horses easy to ride was no virtue of mine, but that, after being bumped and banged about in the train for ten or twelve hours, they would have proved friendly towards anybody who rescued them from their misery and treated them kindly. After petting and talking to them for ten minutes I was their friend for life, and I could do anything with them. They were all horses of great brain and character and taught me a lot, mainly that friendliness and gentleness and firmness can cure any vice.

I was about fourteen when a horse arrived who did not have much brain or character. But what he taught me was fundamental to all my future handling of horses. He was a thoroughbred called The Toff, and we got him because he was completely uncatchable. After we had had him for a week, I decided it was time to teach him to be caught. He was grazing by himself in a two-acre field. I started directly after breakfast, and for the next nine hours I walked after The Toff round and round and up and down the field, and when I walked The Toff walked, always refusing to let me catch him. After the first half-hour he got so bored that he moved only when I got near him; but he still kept walking away, walking away, walking away. This went on for nine hours. But eventually he gave in. He let me catch him and put the halter on. Even at that time I had enough sense to know that the first thing to do when I had caught him was to make a great fuss of him, and the second thing was to turn him loose again. Then for the next hour and a half I walked after The Toff, up the field and down the field, and round and round and round the field again. Then I caught him for the second time and made a fuss of him, and turned him loose. For the next twenty minutes I walked after The Toff, caught him for the third time, made a fuss of him and again turned him loose. I went on like this until I could catch him at my will and turn him loose, and after fourteen hours I went back to have my tea. He taught me one thing: when you start a thing with a horse, you must finish it, no matter what happens. You go on until you have done what you have set out to do, you must have endless patience, never lose your temper, and when he has done what you want, make a fuss of him; and then do it again and again until he does it without question. I do not know what happened to The Toff as he has completely gone from my memory; but I shall always be immensely grateful to him for teaching me what is basic to all my knowledge of handling animals.

Since it was war time, my father, to salve his conscience, made all the horses work on the farm. Thus he could keep horses and feel that he was doing it for the good of the nation rather than for his own pleasure. I remember we had one magnificent thoroughbred gelding called Caravan and he used to have to work in harness and pull one of the farm carts, but he did not approve of it, and used to bolt occasionally, much to everyone's consternation, because he really could travel. I remember driving him out of the yard one day, just as a builder was finishing repairing the gatepost and wall which the horse had demolished when he had bolted only a fortnight before. I drove half a mile down the road and got out to open the gate in the field, only to find that Caravan had swung round, cart and all, and was going flat-out back up the hill. When he got to the yard, the builder, who had just finished the wall, was standing back to admire his work. Caravan came around the corner and the new wall was flat again. The language was blue.

Caravan was a wonderful horse, however, for he had courage as well as determination. During the winter he was sound only one morning a week, and that was the day I was taking him hunting. If on Monday morning I was going hunting, Caravan was sound. He would be lame coming home from hunting and he would be lame until the next hunting day, when he would be sound again. This started me wondering how he knew before he saw me that it was hunting morning.

Of all the mad'ns and bad'ns we had, in fact none was bad, and none was mad. All of them had more than average intelligence, and an awful lot of temper with it. They were horses who had been misunderstood. They were horses who had been ill-treated. They were horses who had been spoilt by kindness. The bad'ns were strong-charactered horses who had been owned by weak-charactered people, and one or two by brutal people. One of them in particular sticks in my mind, a horse called Breakspear, who had a reputation of being a terrible bucker. My father and I went over to Arthur Brake's farm to see him, and my father bought him on the yard. He decided to ride him home. I was fifteen at the time and had broken a leg playing rugger, so had plaster on it from thigh to ankle. My father threw the horse preparatory to mounting him. He was very easy to throw and he behaved himself, did everything perfectly. I remember my father saying that either he was a very bad horse, or there was nothing wrong with him at all. He put his foot in the stirrup and then got on him. Breakspear put on the hell of a buck, my father went up and up and up into the air, then came down and hit the ground very hard. He got on him again and came off him again. After three times he managed to stay on. Then came the problem of getting the car home, so, full of youthful confidence, I said I would drive the car behind my father. I had driven it once or twice about the farm, so I got into the car and proceeded to go in jerks and stalls across the yard of Arthur Brake's farm. By the time I had gone half a mile down the road, my father was waiting for me. He had decided that since he had two more sons at home, he could, if necessary, afford to lose me, but during war time he had no hope of getting another car. So he took me out of the car, and Breakspear, who had had him off another five times in the half-mile, stood absolutely quiet whilst I got on him, one leg stiff in plaster, and took me home as if he was an old plug. He knew I could not do anything if he bucked, so he carried me safely and carefully all the way home. This incident shows the kindness and consideration even the most difficult horse has for a rider who is put in his care.

The horse that followed him displayed the opposite tendency. This was a sixteen-two strawberry-roan mare which we got from the late Arthur Palmer. She was a magnificent horse, but she had one unfortunate tendency: as soon as anyone got on her back, she would go flat out to the nearest tree and try to jam the rider into the trunk or knock him off under the branches. She tried it with me once and got me off. The second time she went straight for a big elm tree, and at the last second, finding I had no hope of steering her away from it, I swung her head the other way hard into the tree so that she went flat-out head-on into the tree. I went flying and she dropped to the ground as if she had been shot. I thought I had killed her. She did not move for about five minutes. When eventually she staggered to her feet very groggily, she was a sadder and wiser horse. I got on her again and rode her around the field, and she never tried that trick on again. But the story shows that an instantaneous reaction, an instant punishment, will cure a horse of most vices. After she had got me off the first time I did not curse at her, I did not swear, I just got on again; but the second time she went into the tree and knocked herself out. When she woke up there I was standing by her talking quietly and gently to her, and after a month or two she lost all desire to hurt human beings, and came to understand that we were her friends.

Early in 1946 my father went to Taunton races. Steeple-chasing had started again just after the war and in the paddock of the three-mile race was a steelpoint gelding called Lucky Bargain. What attracted my father to him was the fact that he bucked his jockey off three times, eventually putting the poor man across the rails so that he could not ride him in the race. My father bought him for £25 from his somewhat disheartened owner. Lucky I will swear could count. It did not matter when you rode him, he always bucked you off three times. After he had had you off three times, he was quite content to let you ride him for the day. He was a very good horse. But he was a horse that taught me to sit a buck, he would twist and turn, and buck in a straight line, he would go flat-out bucking and then he would stop and buck in the same place. He was almost impossible to sit. But at the same time he was an extremely kind and gentle horse, for having bucked you off, he would always wait for you to get on. When you hunted him or raced him he would always give everything he had. He was very generous.

On one occasion my father sold him, warning the man that he bucked, and he went into training. After three months the trainer had had enough and my father bought him back in Exeter market, then we kept him until he died.

Over the next five years I had a number of horses, and through them learnt more and more, because it is only by watching and trying to understand a large number of horses that you can learn what pattern of behaviour is general to each breed, and what is applicable to horses in general rather than to horses in particular.

We had one horse, for instance, who had been completely soured by racing. He was a big chestnut called Tomahawk II and he was French-bred and had won a lot of hurdle races and two-mile steeple-chases. But he had taken a dislike to racing and would refuse to start. He would just run backwards. He could move backwards as fast as many horses could trot, and his trainer and owner had given him up as a bad job and sold him to Bert Newman's son George, who passed him on to me for £15.

I rode him for some time, and on one occasion my wife rode him down to the village of Banscombe, which is half a mile to a mile long, and proceeded down the whole street backwards. We eventually cured him of running backwards by just using patience and not trying to make him go forward. We would sit on him until he wanted to go forward and then he would go forward quite steadily and happily. Within three months we had him going right. He was the sort of horse who really made life worth living: he came to us miserable, unhappy and disliking men in general, but when we passed him on eighteen months later, he was happy, kind and ready to look upon everyone as his friend.

I have always had to sell my horses once they were going right, simply because I have never been able to afford to keep them. My horses have had to keep themselves and help to keep me. But there is another reason why I have allowed horses to come and go. I have always felt that since I have a gift with difficult horses, the gift must be used. If I had concentrated it on one horse and one horse alone, many of the other horses I have had in my life would never have been rehabilitated, and probably ended up in cat-meat tins.

There is one incident in this period that stands out in my mind. I was living down near Lyme Regis at the ne, running a pig farm, and we had five unbroken three-year-olds on the place. One day the hounds met nearby, but I decided not to go out hunting, because my horse was down in the village. I was working on the farm when the hounds found, so I caught the nearest three-year-old and put a bridle on it, and even though it had never been ridden before, it went quietly for me and I hunted it for half an hour until the hounds came back to the farm, and I turned it out. I had hardly turned it out before the hounds found another fox, and since the horse I had been riding was a little tired, I caught the next one of the five – and so on for the rest of the day until I had hunted all five. They all went absolutely quietly, except the fifth, which bucked for about five minutes and that was all, and that taught me a very significant thing: the barrier against riding a horse for the first time is not in the horse, but within the mind of the man who rides him. It is a mental barrier.

In February 1954 I had got married, and in March 1955 my daughter was born. Arguing that the labourer is worthy of some reward, my wife asked me to buy her a horse, so I went down to Exeter market at the beginning of April. I could not see anything I liked at all. I was talking to Arthur Brake, from whom we had bought Breakspear some ten years earlier, when suddenly I heard a commotion, and saw a three-year-old rearing and plunging about. It was being held by two people on the end of a long rope, and the crowd around the ring scattered like confetti. The challenge was too much for me. I bought him for a maiden bid of £27. That horse carried my wife for some twenty years' hunting – we called him Cork Beg after her home – and he proved the horse that taught us most about animal communication.

I will not say much about him here as he will reappear in the pages of the book time and time again. But our relationship had an interesting beginning. I had great difficulty in getting him into the lorry to drive him home, and had to drive him up a cattle chute. When I got home, I unloaded him into the cattle yard to catch him, and noticed that he was frightened about his head and had a very quick temper. So, about two months later, after I had got him riding, I decided I had to make him submit to having his ears touched. I took him out into the yard and got on his back, then I ran my hand up his neck. He threw his head about. I ran my hand up his neck again and he threw his head about again. I kept on doing it for about ten minutes and finally the fragile fragments of his temper went, and he went straight up the road flat-out. Finding he had not worried or dislodged me, he swung to one side and jumped a five-foot barbed-wire fence, landing on the top strand. We both crashed to the ground. I have never been slow to make use of a golden opportunity, so I sat on his head so that he could not get up, and for the next half-hour proceeded to roll my hands all over his head and neck. It did not cure him but he was never quite so bad about his head again, though for years he used to pretend that he was petrified of anyone touching his ears.

For the first four or five years we had him, he was difficult to shoe or clip. When he was being shod the blacksmith, myself and anybody else who was about usually ended up in the yard on the dung heap. As time went on he got better, but for the rest of his life he refused to be shod unless I was there, though for the last ten years I had only to sit and talk to the blacksmith and he would allow himself to be shod.

He was a great character. My wife looked after him herself and I was only asked to help when he was being bloody-minded. Whenever he saw me coming on such an occasion he would gird up his loins for battle, and we would have a battle, enjoyed by both of us. It usually ended with my wife losing her temper and cursing me, but that was all part of the horse. He eventually died at the age of twenty-two.

Nine months before he died, he created what is probably equine history. He was turned out with his current girl-friend – the old man always had to have a girl-friend with him – in a boggy field, and she went across a bog, so he, forgetting his age, decided to follow her, and got himself stuck. When we found him he was half-buried with only his back, head and ears showing. After an hour-and-a-half of hard work, my wife and I managed to roll him on to a piece of dry ground, still in the middle of the bog. It was one of those times: usually when anything goes wrong, there are a thousand people on your doorstep straight away to help, but on this occasion we did not see anyone pass us for nearly two hours, and we were faced with the problem of getting the old man across fifty yards of bog. So I went home and got three five-foot by four-foot sheets of plywood, and made a platform on the bog. The old man was only on three legs, but he managed to hop from the island on to the first piece of plywood, and then on to the second, then on to the third, by which time I had managed to get the first piece in front, and so we went on. Slowly and steadily the old man followed my wife from one piece of plywood to the other. When he was quite sure that it was safe and secure, he would hop on to it. So we got him home. But by this time his back joint was very badly swollen. I thought he must have pulled a tendon in the joint, so we left him hobbling around, and for the next two months, three or four times a day, he would give a screech to let us know that he was lying down and could not get up, and my wife and I would have to go

out. She would take his head and he would get his front
legs up, and I would get under his hind quarters and heave,
until he got his good hind leg from underneath, and could
get up. He never seemed to worry. He would hobble around
quite happily with his girl-friend, and after about five weeks
he was putting his foot to the ground a little bit. By September, about six months later, he was back on his leg again,
though a little stiff in the joint. When the old man died on
17th October we had a post mortem on the leg, and found
that the joint had broken right across and had healed
itself.

A year after I had bought Cork Beg I went back to the market again, looking for a horse myself, and suddenly from a
pen at the back of the market I seemed to get a message:
'for God's sake get me out of this.' I was drawn as if by a
magnet to a sixteen-two-hand dirty brown thoroughbred
horse, who was as thin as a rake. When he came up in the
auction I purchased him for £40. This horse was Weeping
Roger, and he it was who set me seriously to study how
horses communicate with each other and how man communicates with horses.

From the very start Roger and I seemed to have an
affinity for each other, and it was handling and working
him that first made me realize the power a man may
have over a horse, if he really applies his mind to its control
and handling. This set me thinking about the whole question
of communication between man and horse, about how much
it seemed to depend upon *mental* control. If this were
true, conventional training methods were wasteful and in-
efficient.

I decided to test out my ideas. At about this time my
father had bought a four-year-old thoroughbred gelding, who
had been used as a stallion for two years and then castrated,
so I asked him to let me try a new breaking method. I worked
on the horse intensively for seven days: handling him,
gentling him and working him. I got on him on the second
day, and then rode him for an hour in the morning and after-

noon for the next five days. This was a completely unbroken horse, yet on the seventh day we took him down to Taunton, where my father and I were both playing polo, and I was able to play him in a slow chukka and he went extremely well. On the following Wednesday, that is ten days after the horse had first been handled, I played him again, this time in a fast chukka, and he never put a foot wrong. He turned out to be a really first-class polo pony who loved the game.

It normally takes at least two years' schooling to make a polo pony; yet by using mental control to get the horse to want to do what I wanted him to, I had done two years' work in ten days!

I was immensely excited: it seemed to me that I had stumbled on the edge of a real discovery, the meaning of which I was determined fully to grasp. What exactly was the 'mental control' I had exercised over my father's gelding? What precisely was the affinity I felt with Weeping Roger? I was to spend the following years trying to solve these mysteries. Meanwhile I was to have further evidence of the extraordinary sympathy that can exist between human being and horse. One such piece of evidence concerned a pony I bought for my daughter Paddy.

When Paddy was about three years old I went back to Exeter market again, and bought a three-year-old Dartmoor-cross Shetland pony who stood a bare nine hands high. He was obviously too small for me to break, so I got the daughter of a neighbour to break him for me. Darwi (that was his name) and Doreen got on like a house on fire and developed so close an affinity for each other that Darwi, who could get out of any field, whenever he got lonely or bored at night used to take himself the two-and-a-half miles to Doreen and bang on her window until she came to talk to him. Doreen did not mind, but her parents used to object strongly.

Darwi did Paddy extremely well for a couple of years, and then we passed him on to a friend who wanted a child's pony for his daughter. And that was the last we heard of him for eight years. We came to Wales, and Doreen went off to a job somewhere. Then seven or eight years later, my father was at a gymkhana and who should greet him in her rather distinctive voice, but Doreen. My father had not been talking to her for more than five minutes when their attention was drawn to a pony who was whinneying its head off at the far end of the field. Suddenly they could see a pony bolting out of control with a very small child on its back. Child and pony came round the ring flat-out, straight to where my father and Doreen were standing, and skidded to a halt. My father rescued the child, and the pony proceeded to greet Doreen. After eight years he had recognised her voice from the other side of the field. I do not suppose Doreen had handled Darwi for more than three or four months. But a bond was there between them even after eight years.

These experiences redoubled my enthusiasm for the work we were beginning to do on animal communication, and encouraged me to start trying to make some sense out of the signs, sounds and other signals we could observe the horses using to make their intentions and wishes plain to each other.

2: *Horses in History – Man's Unique Bond with the Horse*

Basic communication with horses is quite simple, and there is nothing superhuman about it. The horse can easily be trained to communicate with man, and to understand man's communication. If you sit on a horse and pull the reins, it will stop quite easily – it is trained to stop when it feels the pressure of the bit. When you touch it with your heels it will go forward. You can steer it to the right, you can steer it to the left. You can teach your horse very quickly to do anything it is physically capable of doing. This is all communication, because man is communicating to the horse through a language which they both understand, a language of signs taught to the horse by man.

But the horse himself also communicates with other horses, and it is this communication that I have set out to understand. Over the past twenty years I have concentrated my energies on grasping the language that horses use themselves, not only to understand other horses but to communicate also with man. For I was convinced that there is another and more subtle level of communication between man and horse than the simple pressure of heel and rein. But of course I realized that before I could do anything, I had to understand how much was already known to man.

I was between twelve and fourteen when I first started to wonder why man rode horses and not cattle, sheep or pigs, and so I experimented a little. I tried to ride the heifers and pigs on the farm, and after being deposited a great number of times on the ground, concluded that the reason they were so difficult to ride was that they would simply not co-operate and work *with* you as horses do. Yet this conclusion itself poses a problem: *why* would horses let you ride them and not other animals? It was obvious that the horse was more intelligent than either the cow or the pig. It was just as obvious that it was stronger. Yet cattle are much more docile than horses, they drive more easily, they are quieter and steadier and much safer animals to handle. Yet you cannot ride them. It could not be an instinct of self-preservation which made the heifer shake the rider off its back, since the same animal preyed on both the cattle and the horse. I could only suppose that there was some unique rapport, a special relationship, between man and horse which does not exist with any other animal, excepting possibly the dog. Why this should be so I did not know at the time, but I was to find out later from reading and from my own experience.

From my reading I discovered that horses featured in the cave drawings of prehistoric man first as prey for food, and later as mounts for man in hunting and in battle. Pictures of horses are engraved on the tombs of the Pharaohs, horses are embodied in the Greek myths. Greek sculptors carved horses on their magnificent friezes. It was Xenophon, the famous Greek general, who said: 'horses are taught not by harshness but by gentleness.'

Alexander the Great was able to conquer a great part of the then known world largely by his use of his fine cavalry; and he it probably was who first discovered the value of crossing the hot-blooded Arab with the cold-blooded horse of Europe. His closeness to his own mount is shown by the fact that his horse Bucephalus is one of the first to be mentioned by name in history.

The great myth of the centaurs who were supposed to be part man, part horse was probably based on travellers' reports of the Mongolian tribe, the Hsiung-nu, who were later to appear as the Huns under Attila who tore the Roman Empire apart. The Hsiung-nu were nomads who controlled the whole of the central and Eastern European plain and were herdsmen and warriors. They kept their herds on the oceans of grass extending from the Hungarian plain to Manchuria and the great wall of China. Always searching for food, in the winter they sheltered under the lee of the mountains and in the spring they moved north and east to find fresh grazing. They waged war on everybody, even on sections of their own race, and on all of the northern civilized world. They were said to be born on horseback and could ride before they could walk. They used their horses for everything: they would no more think of walking more than two or three steps than they would dream of flying, and so no doubt gave rise to the legend of a race that were part man and part horse.

By the end of the second century BC the Hsiung-nu ruled a large section of the world. The Emperor of China, Wu-ti, was in such terror of them that he developed a very formidable cavalry force, and about 142 BC the brilliant Chinese General Hoc'u-P'ing managed to split the main Hsiung-nu army; but even then the Chinese cavalry proved inferior. So the Emperor Wu-ti sent an army of three hundred thousand men three thousand miles to Western Afghanistan to capture a superior breed of horse. The whole army died on the way. Nothing daunted, Wu-ti sent out a second army, and enough of these survived the three thousand miles to Afghanistan and three thousand miles back to bring back thirty breeding animals. They were probably a strain of Arab, reported to be able to travel three hundred miles a day and to sweat blood. Almost certainly they were descendants of Arabs who had been carried eastwards by Alexander the Great's troops.

The success of Julius Caesar in establishing Roman rule over so much of Europe was almost certainly due to his brilliance as a cavalry general. Again, he and his horse were reported to be inseparable. The Emperor Caligula, indeed, thought so much of his horse Incitatus that, according to legend, he made him a Senator, claiming that he was both wiser and more loyal than any other member of the Senate. The Roman Empire survived 500 years, until the superior horse power of the Hun army, which had already conquered the northern world, finally sacked Rome in AD 408.

Later these same Mongolian horseback tribes were to reappear as the hordes of Ghengis Khan, who were also supposed to be conceived, born and married, and finally to die,
on their horses. On one occasion Ghengis Khan's troops
conquered a town by climbing a cliff on horseback which the
defenders thought to be unscalable by man.

Central to all this history lies the uncanny relationship
between man and horse. Later Norman knights in armour
and the fabulous Ottoman cavalry took their turns to conquer
the then-known world. In each case a key to victory was the
understanding and use of the horse; for these ancient armies
were made up of riders who knew how to communicate with
horses.

There is a story told of an Arab chief named Jabal who
owned the fastest horse in the world. Hassad Pacha, then
governor of Damascus, wished to buy the mare and repeatedly
made Jabal the most liberal offers, which he steadily refused.
The Pacha threatened him but with no better success. In the
end he persuaded a Bedouin called Gafar, from another
tribe, to steal the mare, offering as a reward to fill the mare's
nosebag with gold. News of this bargain got out and Jabal
became more watchful than ever and secured his mare at
night with an iron chain, one end of which was fastened to
her hind fetlock and the other to the ground under Jabal's
bed. But one night Gafar crept silently into the tent and
succeeded in loosening the chain. Just before he started off
with the mare, he caught up Jabal's lance and poking him
with the butt end, cried out 'I am Gafar, I have stolen your
noble mare and give you notice in time.' This warning was in
accordance with the customs of the desert, for to rob a
member of another tribe was considered to be an honourable
exploit, and Gafar wanted the glory of the theft. Jabal when
he heard the words rushed out of the tent and gave the
alarm, jumped on to his brother's horse and, accompanied
by some of his tribe, pursued the robber for four hours. The
brother's mare was of the same breeding as Jabal's horse, but
was not quite as fast as she was. Nevertheless she out-galloped

all the other pursuers and was on the point of overtaking
the robber, when Jabal shouted at him 'pinch her right ear
and give her the touch of the heel.' Gafar did so and went away
with the mare like lightning, speedily rendering pursuit hope-
less. The pinch of the ear and the touch of the heel were the
secret signs by which Jabal had been used to make his mare
increase her speed. Jabal's companions were amazed and
indignant at his strange conduct. 'You are the father of a
jackass,' they cried, 'Fancy enabling the thief to rob you!'
But he answered them by saying 'I would rather lose her than
spoil her reputation. Would you have me suffer it to be said
among the tribes that another mare had proved greater than
mine? I have at least this comfort left to me. I can say she
has never met her match.'

This is a lovely legend, and the point of it is that until
the correct form of communication was used, the mare
did not know what to do, but as soon as the correct command was given, she settled down and galloped like the
wind.

In America too there are countless stories of the horse,
but the only American Indians who set out to study and
understand the horse were the Mohicans. They did not break
the horse's spirit by getting on it and riding it until it gave in.
They used to spend days handling it, talking to it and feeding
it, and gently, gently, gently getting on its back. They would
work for hours over a horse's back with a blanket, and when
the horse understood what they wanted, they had no trouble
in riding it.

Over the last century there have been men all over the
world who have gained fame as horse-tamers. In America
there was Reary, in Australia Galvin, in Ireland Dan Sullivan
the Whisperer, and in this country Palmer and later on Captain Hayes. The stories about them are legion, but basically
they have one feature in common, and this is the hero's
ability to control and dominate a horse no matter how difficult or how wild. Their methods varied. Reary had a system
of ropes and throwing a horse to train it. Galvin had a

number of 'humane twitches', as he called them. Some, like Palmer, had 'taming oils', for which there were various recipes, one involving grinding the chestnut of a horse's leg into a powder, and blowing it into his nostrils. Oil of rhodium was sometimes used, so was origanum, and some people simply used the sweat from their armpits. These techniques have one virtue in common : they all gave the person using them a certain amount of confidence in handling a difficult horse.

But Sullivan the Horse-Whisperer was probably the greatest of all the old-fashioned horse tamers, for he used nothing but his own ability. He would go up to horses, who were killers, kickers or unbreakable in some other way, and he would have the door shut on him. After an hour or so he would open the door, and walk the horse out on a halter absolutely quiet. The Whisperer never took any pupils and he never taught even his own sons his skill. He was so jealous of his gift that even his priest at Ballyclough could not get the secret out of him in confession. Sullivan's sons used to boast about how His Reverence met the Whisperer on the road towards Mallow and charged him with being a confederate of the devil. The Whisperer made the priest's horse bolt for miles until the holy man promised in despair to let Sullivan alone with his secret for ever. Only one of the Whisperer's sons practised his art, but he had no real knowledge of how to do it and neither of the other two pretended any skill at all. The Whisperer had a great fascination for me because I had this ability to handle difficult horses myself, and I often wondered how his gift compared with mine. But I think he used something similar to the system that we practice ourselves when we gentle a horse. I believe he used to get his hand on to the horse and simulate the movements of a mare nuzzling her foal, and as soon as the horse understood the familiar signs, he would relax, and all the time Sullivan would be talking with his gentle sing-song Irish voice, until he could get both his hands on the horse and relax him, and create a bond of understanding between him and the horse.

Palmer, the English horse-tamer, used taming oils which he would put on his hand, then put his hand under the horse's nose and blow it up his nostrils, and the horse would immediately become docile. Barbara Woodhouse relates how a similar practice is still used in South America, though without the oils, probably taken there from this country about the middle of the last century. There is nothing strange about this custom: when two horses meet, they will blow through their nostrils, strongly or gently depending on their mood. Two horses that are hostile to each other will almost trumpet through their nostrils; while a mare caressing her foal will blow so gently that you can hardly hear her. When Palmer blew up the horse's nostrils, all he said was 'I am friendly, I will not hurt you.' If you are doing this yourself you should next get your hand on to the horse and get your fingers into physical contact. The horse again will understand; because when two horses are frightened, they will push together to get physical contact.

This principle is similar to that behind the system practised by the American Mohicans. They too would get physical contact with their horses, and as soon as physical contact was established the horse began to understand, because the signs that he used himself were being used.

It should now be clear that these methods all had one thing in common: they all used the signs that the horses use themselves, and so instead of using foreign signs and sounds to train a horse, they used signs and sounds the horse already understood.

Captain Horace Hayes' methods are so well known that there is no need for me to go into them here, but the point of interest is that a pupil of his was Captain Ward Jackson, who was my father's Company Commander in India during the First World War, and Ward Jackson took my father as a pupil and taught him Hayes' methods, and in turn of course my father taught me, so I always feel a very close contact with Horace Hayes. There is a lovely story about him, which as far as I know has not been told before. When Hayes was in India he dined one night in a neighbouring mess. The wine was good and it was well sampled, the whole party got rather high, and everyone was talking expansively. Now it so happened that the Colonel of the regiment owned an unmanageable horse and late in the evening he sold it to Hayes, and then bet him that he would be unable to ride him on parade the next day. They settled for a bet of five hundred rupees. Horace Hayes, anxious to win his bet, left the party and spent the rest of the night working on the horse to get it going. The following morning Hayes rode the horse out on parade, and the horse went beautifully for him. The Colonel, anticipating the loss of his five hundred rupees, ordered the troops to fire a *feu-de-joie*, which meant that they fired off their rifles at random. When this happened all the other chargers disappeared with their riders over the horizon; but not so the horse Hayes was riding. He stood like a rock, still and relaxed. As soon as the order was given, Hayes had kicked his feet out of the stirrups, pulled out his pipe and lit it. He was so relaxed that his horse took no notice of the rifles being fired. The other officers on the other hand, fearing that the horses were going to bolt, pulled them together, and in doing so, frightened them even more than the rifles had done. This story finely illustrates the great control that man can have over a horse by controlling him mentally as well as physically.

Such control and understanding no doubt not only applies to horses, for it is probably the great art of stockmanship in general to know and understand the animals that you are handling and sense when something is wrong with them. I remember an incident that took place when I was about twelve years old. By some miracle I had beaten Les the cowman into the cowshed one morning. (This was the only time it ever happened that I was up before Les.) I remember him coming into the cow stall, and almost before he was through the door, saying 'What is the matter with Pride?' He could not see Pride, but sure enough, when he walked down to the far end of the cow stall, Pride was lying down with milk fever. There was a bond between Les and the cows of much the same kind as I feel with horses.

Similarly, a shepherd may have an intuitional sympathy with his sheep. I have heard a shepherd claim that at lambing time he often got up in the middle of the night, without quite knowing why, to go out to the sheep; and to use his own words 'Hardly a journey was a wasted one.' There was always something wrong that needed his attention.

Animal communication has become a problem of increasing concern to modern mankind over the past twenty years. The Russians were the first people to start serious research just over twenty years ago, and more recently the Americans have taken an interest. The Russians however, seem to have started off on the wrong track. They based their work on observations on dogs and rats and the thing that I think led them the wrong way is the fact that the rat has a number of signals with definite meanings, that are easy to discern, and researchers have thus been encouraged to try to make patterns of other signals and sounds, or of the signs made by other animals. For example, the rat has a definite signal for distress and other signals for alarm : these are vocal signals designed to carry a very large distance. It also has an ultrasonic squeak which it gives when meeting another rat, the note of the squeak denoting its place within the social hierarchy. The dog equally has a number of sounds which have definite meanings. But to observe these sounds without taking into account other forms of communication leads only to a dead-end. They are only *part* of the animal's communication system.

The Americans have done a lot of very good work, though they have also concentrated on sounds. Their work was on dolphins, however, whose main form of communication is in sound : because a lot of dolphin communication takes place when the animals are out of sight of each other, the dolphins seem to have a developed vocal language which most animals do not.

This primary mistake of the early researchers, who tried to make a pattern out of the sounds the animals made, was largely the result of assuming that man's behaviour pattern was similar in this respect to that of animals. Since people of the same race use a set language it was argued that man as a whole uses a set language, which he does not. Mankind as a whole uses a number of languages. It was also assumed that man communicates using sounds alone, and this again is wrong. Man does not use sounds alone to convey any meaning, since he also uses signs and facial expression, which itself is a sign. The major error in these three basic assumptions has resulted in only part of each animal's language being investigated – that is, only sounds or signs – and it is obviously impossible to understand any language by only understanding part of it.

As we will show later, man's behaviour pattern in communication cannot be directly related to forms of comunication used by animals. Each species of animal is different. You cannot conclude that the form of communication used by one species is in any way parallel to the form of communication used by a completely different species. Very fortunately in this country, the little research that has been done in communication has been done in conjunction with research into animal behaviour. This has meant that research has not followed the pattern that has dominated the Russians and the Americans. Doctor Martha Kylie has done some research with cattle, and Meek and Ewbank have done a certain amount of research at Liverpool University. (In a similar spirit some very good work has been done in Africa on apes and chimpanzees.) Very little practical use has been made so far of any of this research into animal communication, however.

The Americans on the other hand have used their research to train dolphins for military purposes, and incidentally for use in the movies. The film *The Day of the Dolphin* is a fascinating example of how research into animal communication can be used. The six dolphins in this film were

caught by the trainer Peter Moss off the coast of Florida. He
was to remark later that there was something more than a
man-animal relationship in the situation that developed
between George C. Scott, who was the star of the film, Mike
Nicolls, who was the director, and the dolphins. So great
was this rapport that one observer who watched the dolphins
at work insisted that the the dolphins were actually 'expressing
themselves' – that they really could act. Nicolls himself said
he found himself reacting to the dolphins just as if they were
temperamental actors. Some days he loved them, some days
he hated them. Since the dolphins' life is all play, their
favourite game was rearranging the underwater lights used
in the film, which at times made the filming impossible.
Nicolls would get furious with them when they refused to do
something they knew how to do, but then two minutes later
they would come and rub their bellies on his feet and nibble
his toes as if saying, to use his words, 'come on, don't be
mad'. On one occasion Nicolls was sitting by the pool
reading the script for the next day's scene, with one hand
lightly scratching the tongue of the dolphin who was playing
the male lead. The dolphin had been christened Buck, and
Buck just lay there with his head on the side of the tank
and his mouth wide open. Then Nicolls looked at Buck,
and suddenly knew he was ready to be filmed. Right on cue
the dolphin swam to the side of the tank, pushed himself
under the arm of the boy who was playing the scene with
him, and then proceeded to dive and swim right through a
narrow opening, still with the boy in tow. Such was his timing
that he got the actor to the position right on cue to say his
two lines. In all, Buck and the actor repeated the movement
ten times, but each time they were failed by sunlight. Then
on the eleventh attempt, Buck, who had not made a mistake
throughout, reared out of the water, began to make a series
of sounds which built up into a noise like a football cheer,
turned abruptly and swam away. 'That was what I was
afraid of,' said Moss, 'it was boring him.'

Peter Moss had no trouble in teaching the dolphins to

perform specific actions. But when one of the dolphins had to have a worried, apprehensive look, that was more difficult. In the end it was Nicolls who taught the dolphins to look apprehensive. Moss himself says that if he described the relationship that grew up between the dolphins and the director, people would say that he was mad.

It had been decided that at the end of the film the dolphins would be allowed to go free. Nicolls said that in the event there was no choice about it: as soon as the two main dolphins had finished their last shot they made their own decision, turned round and swam out to the ocean. They took care of their fate themselves; but only when they knew the film was finished.

This story may be dismissed as a typical piece of Publicity Office ballyhoo, but to anyone who has experienced the amazing results that can be obtained by communicating with animals in the language that they understand, and developing a real relationship with them, it has that unmistakable ring of truth. There are things in the story that even Hollywood could not dream up: even in this permissive age to suggest that one of its directors and a male dolphin could form a special relationship, is a little outrageous!

I was reminded by this story of something that happened to me in 1970 at the Royal Welsh Show. The Welsh Cob Society had been asked to put on a display in the main ring and I was to do a special demonstration at the end, showing the versatility of the Welsh Cob. I had an awkward bloody-minded little horse called Trefais Comet. He was also without any doubt one of the most versatile horses of the breed, and I had developed a tremendous relationship with him. For the demonstration I had prepared a number of exercises, one of which was a full pass, which means that the horse walks at right angles to itself sideways. When I tried to teach him this, I took him up to a four-foot forestry fence, walked him up the fence once sideways then down sideways and then up sideways again. I was feeling very pleased with myself, so I decided to do it once more. I went down sideways, then he

took half a step back and went straight over the four-foot
fence and that was that. I decided I could not do it at the
Royal Welsh. But on the first day we had a wait before the
display, so I was thinking about this when Comet suddenly,
without any prompting from me, did a full pass one way
and a full pass the other, and so that went into the demonstration. On the second day I was asked beforehand what I was
going to do, so I told the officials, and Comet went straight
into the ring and did everything exactly as I said I was
going to do it, plus something that I would have thought was
impossible, which was jumping into the air and turning in
the air to face in the opposite direction. After his performance,
he so loved the crowd's applause that he proceeded to invent
things for himself to excel in. He was very fast and excitable, and one of the things I knew I could not do was
stop him dead, but nevertheless he finished his demonstration
completely out of control, galloping straight towards the
president's box and then at the last second stopping dead
and standing on his hind legs. I had wanted him to do this
and he knew I had wanted to do it, so he put it in himself.
This is the kind of phenomenon that is possible once you are
communicating with your horse effectively.

In the early days of our work, which began in 1955–6,
we dealt mainly with Weeping Roger and Cork Beg. This
meant that our research was largely limited to the signs and
sounds used by those two particular horses. We knew that
there was more to 'Equine Communication' than signs and
sounds, but we felt it best to begin by trying to understand
what the horse was saying, and why and how he responded to
the signs and sounds used by another horse. This knowledge
would be the basis for future work. But it was soon obvious
from our observations that the horses were using the same
signs and same sounds to convey a large number of meanings, so we concluded that there must be something more
than signs and sounds at work to distinguish one meaning
from another, and we called this unknown factor 'attitude'

or 'feeling'. It was only later that we used the terms 'telepathy' and 'extra-sensory perception' : in fact it was ten
years before we came round to doing so.

Research into the communication between animals is of
comparatively recent origin, but knowledge and understanding of animal communication is as old as man himself, and
primitive tribes today have far more knowledge of animal
communication than civilized man. Laurens Van Der Post in
his travels among the bushmen discovered that the witch
doctors could put themselves into a trance by gazing at the
cave drawing of an antelope, and then describe where the
antelope were to be found. In other words, the witch doctor
could put himself in mental communication with any antelope
within ten or fifteen miles' radius, so that the hunters of the
tribe could go out and kill it for food. Van Der Post calls
this facility 'empathy'. But from our own work, we know it to
be the one we call telepathy : the ability that animals use to
transfer mental pictures to one another.

Much modern research into animal communication has
been complicated by the fact that it has been limited to only
one means of communication, usually sound; and this is as
fruitless as trying to understand English by learning only
the verbs. If we are to understand what horses are trying to
say, and to make ourselves easily understood by them, we
must use and understand the whole language, and not just
one part of it. We must thus learn to think and react as the
horse thinks and reacts, and guard against the sentimentality
of anthropomorphism : that is, against endowing the animal
with human characteristics. Indeed the man must reverse the
process and when handling horses become half-horse. Alex
Kerr, the lion tamer, was once asked if he would allow his
daughter to tame and train big cats, and he said no. Asked
why, he said, 'Well, it is quite simple. To do it successfully
she must think like a lion or a tiger, and if she thinks and
acts like a lion or a tiger, the lion or tiger will look upon her
as a lion or tiger, and that would mean that when she came
into season, as human beings do just as animals do, the cat

would know. And since the way a lion denotes affection is to pick the female up by the scruff of the neck, that is what he would do. And he would break her neck.' This is the essence of our communicating work. Alex Kerr probably had more understanding of how felines think than any living man and his book *No Bars Between* is unequalled.

The first person in recent times to claim to be able to communicate with animals was the Englishman Archie Delany, who masqueraded for a long time as an Indian half-breed called Grey Owl and wrote two famous books, *Tales of an Empty Cabin* and *Sasho and the Beaver People*. He was also the first man to advocate conservation, and he started the first of the modern nature reserves. Although in some things he was a fraud, he was also a very great man with a very great understanding with wild animals, especially beavers, on whose habits and behaviour patterns he did some outstanding work. The beavers accepted him so completely that they made their lodge within his cabin at the side of a lake. He claimed to have produced a dictionary of beaver language, but I have unfortunately not been able to obtain a copy of this dictionary, and those reports I have of it indicate that it has been of little use to other people.

One of the many people to visit him was Mr John Diefenbaker, later Canadian Prime Minister, who visited him in late 1935 or early 1936. When he got there with a party of people, Delany said he would have to go and ask the beavers if they would receive him. Then he came back and said that the beavers had said they would. This was obviously pure showmanship, but there is little doubt that in spite of his masquerade Delany did make a magnificent breakthrough in the study of animal communication. It was nearly twenty years before anyone else even attempted to communicate with animals, and very little use has been made of his work, mainly, I suspect, because of the academic's inbuilt prejudice against any research done by a person living and working outside a university. But it is my feeling that it is to people like Alex Kerr and Grey Owl that we have to turn if we wish to extend our present understanding of animal communication and behaviour.

There is a real difficulty in this experiential approach to study. For to understand the horse you must become a horse, you must think like a horse and act like a horse, research becomes extremely difficult, since it is difficult to be analytical at the same time as trying to think and react as the animals will do: animals are simply not analytical! But we are not, nor have we ever been, concerned with orthodox research. We are interested only in gaining a greater understanding of our horses, and we hope that other people will reap from the ground that we are now sowing. It will be for them to take the work that we have done and analyse it, and carry out orthodox research on the foundations that we are now building.

3: *The Language of Horses*

It is already clear that there is a great deal of communication between man and horse in the ordinary process of handling. First man communicates with a horse with his voice in his basic training of his animal. He teaches him certain words of command: 'whoa,' 'walk on,' 'trot on,' 'steady,' and so on. These words the horse learns and his rider hopes that he will obey them. In turn, man learns the significance of some of the sounds used by the horse. He quickly learns to recognize the whicker of welcome, the neigh saying 'is anybody about,' and the squeal of anger.

Man also teaches his horse a number of signs: he touches the horse with his heels to tell him to go forward and he pulls at the reins, that is he exerts pressure on the horse's mouth, to make him stop. He caresses him when the horse is good and he hits him when he has done wrong. These exchanges are all basic to communicating with any animal. A vet trying to diagnose an illness will observe other signs made by a horse: for instance if a place hurts the horse will wince if you touch it. The horse will also tell you if you are hurting him by a sharp intake of breath. You can also tell if the horse is sick and out of sorts by his listless and dejected attitude. All these are the ways a horse communicates by signs with you. He will equally tell you if he is excited and he will tell you if he is tired, by the way he carries himself.

When we started research into animal communication, we decided to try to compile a short dictionary of horse messages, and for this we started by following the path that had been trodden by most people in the same field. Since we use sounds ourselves to communicate, it seemed obvious to start by studying horse sounds, so we decided to try to deduce some pattern from the sounds horses make. In these

42

early stages we had a certain degree of success. We found that the whicker of welcome and the neigh of alarm were sounds that were common to very nearly all horses. But the more research we carried out, the more we discovered that we could not rely on set patterns as a guide to interpreting the sounds used by horses as a species. It became clear that different horses use the same sequence of sounds to convey different meanings, each horse having its own language, only similar to that of its associates and not identical. So we had to go back and start again.

We did this first by looking at how human beings communicate, and we discovered that as much is conveyed by the tone of voice and the manner of delivering a phrase as by the actual words themselves. For example, an Englishman, an Irishman, a Scotsman and a Welshman all speak English. They can understand each other, but their means of conveying any meaning is different. They will use different words, different phrases in different forms. In other words, people of different cultural background, even though they speak the same basic language, will use different words and phrases to convey a single meaning. And even within one culture, people of different nature and temperament will use divergent word-forms to convey a single meaning. Certain sounds on the other hand are standard to all people of the same race and are used at certain times: the word 'hello' for instance is common to all English-speaking people. It is in the same sense that the whicker of welcome is common to all horses. And just as the cry of 'help' is used by all people who speak English, most horses have a neigh or scream of alarm.

We also looked at the importance of the tone of voice to meaning. We found that the tone of the voice used by human beings to convey a standard message can vary both its meaning and its force. For example, a man or a woman using the phrase 'come here' can vary its whole sense by the tone of voice. If the words are murmured by a woman in a soft and seductive voice, it can be an invitation to make love. If the tone of voice is sharp or harsh it is a command to be obeyed instantly, and if screamed 'come here' can be a cry for help. In the same way the horse can vary its message by a raising and hardening of the voice, so that similar sounds can mean anything from 'come here, darling' to, in its highest and hardest imperative, 'if you do not come here immediately I will have your guts for garters.' And exactly the same message can be used as a cry for help.

The second thing we found we had to take into account was that habits of communication vary according to sex; and whereas among human beings there are only two sexes, male and female, among domesticated horses there are three sexes, male, female and neuter. This is important, since the note and tone of each sex is different: the range of notes used by a stallion and a mare are completely different, and the gelding will come somewhere between the two. This is not so important when you are in contact with a single horse, but it is extremely important to remember if you are handling a large number of horses, or are trying to understand what a strange horse is saying, since the same sequence of notes used by a mare, a gelding and a stallion can mean different things.

Before you can even start to interpret a message made by sound, therefore, you have to know the sex of the animal. We also discovered that it is important to take into account the age of the horse, because obviously the range of tones and notes used by a foal is completely different from the notes and range he will use as a stallion four or five years later.

On the other hand the stallion, mare, gelding, foal and yearling will all have the same number of tones and notes, and they will be made in eleven different ways. Nine of the eleven different tones of voice are made by exhaling, that is to say they are made by breathing out. First there is a snort, which is made by using the nostrils alone as a sound box, and at times the imperative is expressed by crackling the nostrils at the same time. The stronger note with the crackling of the nostrils is used to draw attention as a signal of alarm, as a sign the horse is excited or to denote strong emotions.

The whicker is also made by using the nostrils as a sound box, but this is a much more caressing note and can vary from a very gentle blowing through the nostrils to quite a strong sound, used usually as a greeting or to show affection of some sort. Then there is the whinney, which is a much higher-pitched enquiring sound, and the neigh, which is stronger again than the whinney. In these two the voice box is used. In addition we know the squeal of the mare, and the bell of the stallion, each of which can have a distinctive sexual tone to them, or may sound aggressive or be used as a warning. These both come from the upper nasal regions of the voice box and are used in sex play, in anger or to display temper. The stallion has a whistle which he uses to call the mare; and all horses have a scream of fear, pain or anger which comes as a gust of terror from the lungs. These are all exhaling sounds. The breathing-in sounds consist of a snuffle, which corresponds to the gentle blowing out, and a sniff, which corresponds to the snort. Each of these notes has a definite meaning for another horse.

The stallion has the greatest vocal range, and some of his notes are frightening, while others will be very beautiful to hear. But he has a somewhat limited range of messages to deliver with his voice, simply because in his natural state he is concerned only with three things: sex, danger and food. So his messages are confined to these three subjects. In fact you might say he has only got three subjects of conversation, fear, food and female, which makes him very like man, except that man has one further topic of conversation, and that is how best to avoid work. So in addition to 'let's eat', 'let's make love', 'let's bugger off', mankind also adds 'let's strike'!

A mare on the other hand, while she has her sexual sounds and her sounds for food and danger, also has a range of sounds for the care and protection of her foal, and probably her yearling as well. She has to call her young to her for food, she has to call them in case of threatened danger and she has to teach them discipline, so her range of messages will be far greater than that of the stallion. A gelding, which

of course does not exist in the wild, has a vocal range which
may vary from that of a stallion, if it has been cut very late,
to that of a mare if it is over-protective to the person who
looks after it. A foal equally will have its own messages and
vocal range concerning food and fear; it will have no sexual
messages but it will have a range of sounds asking for protection and reassurance, and these will change as he gets
older. He will retain some of his foal phrases as a yearling and
even as a two-year-old. Then, when he starts feeling a man
in his two-year-old summer, and certainly as a three-year-old,
unless he has already been cut, his messages and voice will
change to that of a stallion; or a filly will develop the language
of a mare.

Contact with man too increases a horse's vocal range.
This makes for complications, since it is almost impossible
to differentiate between the messages that are natural to the
horse and those that result from contact with man. If feeding
is late, for example, a horse that has been in contact with
man will whinney or bang his manger, or make some other
sign to remind you it is time to feed him. This action is
completely unknown to the horse in the wilds, since his food
is always there, and he does not have to draw man's attention to the fact that he is hungry. We note from observation that when a horse discovers the messages that he is trying
to convey are understood, either by another horse or by
man, he will use it again: that is, he extends his own
vocabulary. The most extensive vocabulary we have ever
come across was that of Cork Beg whom we owned for twenty
years, and we observed that other horses who had had little
or no contact with man learned phrases from him and thus
extended their vocabularies.

We were taught just how much one horse can learn
from another by another horse belonging to my wife, Rostellan.
When Cork Beg was getting somewhat arthritic and stiff
and no longer enjoyed a long day's hunting, it was important
to get another horse to help him out. We were very fortunate in that we had a registered Welsh Cob, Trefais Dafydd,

who seemed to fill the bill perfectly. Trefais Dafydd being such a mouthful, we called him Rostellan after an estate near my wife's home in Ireland. (Cork Beg had been named after her home.) He arrived at our place in a lorry-load of nine horses, none of which had ever been handled in any way. He was a big, black three-year-old. By the autumn, when we decided to keep him, he had filled out considerably and had established his own particular place in the establishment. The only way my wife could find time to exercise two horses during the winter was to ride Cork Beg and let Rostellan follow behind with her labrador, Dora. He soon learnt to follow very closely to heel and never tried to pass Cork Beg. If he did Cork Beg would swing his head round and threaten to have a large piece of his anatomy for breakfast. Having established the correct order in the herd of two, Cork Beg was quite pleased to take on an apprentice and to teach him the tricks of the trade, and just how much the pupil was learning from the master I discovered one day when I went out after lunch. Cork Beg had a habit of standing with his head out of the stable door with his bottom lip flapping in the wind. This particular day was a nice sunny day and I came round the corner, and there were the pair of them, Rostellan imitating Cork Beg with his lip flapping completely relaxed. Rostellan had added his own touch to it by sticking two inches of tongue out as well.

Some things however were not quite so easy to teach. For example Cork Beg had a habit of standing with his hind legs crossed, that is with one hind leg resting in front of the other. The only time Rostellan tried it he ended up sitting on his bottom in a very undignified position, and he did not try that particular trick again. But mostly Cork Beg concentrated on teaching Rostellan the things he needed to know : for example he taught him exactly what he had to do when my wife was depressed. She, as everyone else, at times feels the weight of the world very heavy on her shoulders, and on these occasions she used to take Cork Beg out and Cork

Beg would proceed through a whole gamut of tricks to make her laugh. The first one he would try on going out through the gate was to make a dive at Dora, who used to bark, pretending to bite his nose. Then he would walk sedately down the road until he saw a convenient object to shy at. He would shy right across the road as if it was the most terrifying think he had ever seen. It might be a fencing post or it might be a leaf blowing along the road, or a robin flying out of a fence, but Cork Beg would react to it with one bound and jump from one side of the road to the other, and stand cowering and shivering in the ditch. If this did not succeed in cheering my wife up a little bit, he used to take even sterner measures. He would wait until there was a grassy stretch on the roadway, then he would jump forward in a series of bounds, and gallop off in pursuit of Dora. Having gone five or six strides and made sure my wife was quite firm in the saddle, he used to proceed to put in a series of four or five bucks. I have even seen him on occasion, when he had unseated my wife, dodge to one side on landing and catch her as she came down. This trick was almost infallible, because he would not stop bucking until he had her laughing.

One of the greatest advantages we have for working a horse is the fact that we live on the edge of 2,000 acres of Forestry Commission land, where we have the benefit of any number of grassy rides. One of the things the old man loved doing was to walk along pretending to be half asleep until he came to the corner of one of these rides, then he would suddenly dodge to one side round the corner and dash flat out as fast as he could with Dora in pursuit, and this was another infallible trick for making my wife laugh. One of the amazing things about him was that no matter how arthritic and stiff he was, even after he had broken his leg, he still used to go through the whole gamut of his tricks, and after doing them he would dance along as if he was a completely unmanageable and unschooled three-year-old.

Another thing he had to teach Rostellan was of course that

whenever I appeared on the scene in the stable, set on doing something, he had to put up a show of being a wild unmanageable horse, completely terrified of the boss. I could go into the stable fifty times to do my stable chores, and have a job to get the old man to move over. But if I went in with a brush to groom him, to get the worst of the mud off after a day's hunting, then it was a case of battle stations.

Yet another thing the old man had to teach Rostellan was that when you are competing, if the missus was on board everyone was out to enjoy themselves. It was not important whether you won a prize or not, provided a good time was had by all. But when the boss got on you were really competing and you had to get down to it and give every ounce you had. I used to compete with the old man once or twice a year and I never took him anywhere without winning a prize with him. He was placed three times point-to-pointing, won several hunter trials, and I even used to play polo on him. He was an absolutely superb horse.

Whilst Rostellan was not as intelligent as Cork Beg and was built differently, being a Welsh Cob instead of a three-quarter thoroughbred, he was a very willing pupil and over the course of the next three years he learnt most of what Cork Beg could teach him. This was a case where over a period of time one horse took on part of the personality of another.

The story of how Rostellan's character was changed by the influence of my wife and Cork Beg is only one example of how the character and behaviour pattern of a horse can be completely altered by a change in environment. And an alteration in the horse's environment has of course considerable consequence for equine communication, since change in his needs and habits means also that the horse needs a new and extended vocabulary to meet these new demands. Perhaps I can best explain what I mean in human terms. I live on Llanybyther mountain in North Carmarthenshire, my neighbours are farmers, as I was myself at one time, and the topics of conversation are horses, hunting, the weather, sheep and cattle, in that order – together with the latest bit of local gossip of course. The words we use are relevant to these subjects. Now if I were to move to London or the Midlands and take a job in an office or a factory, the topics of my conversation would change to football, cricket, cars, the theatre and music, and I would use words and phrases which at present I never use. Equally, when horses are in their natural environment they live within a group with a fixed pattern of behaviour and a distinct social structure, descending from the lead mare to the lowliest yearling – the stallion will be outside the herd, usually unattached temporarily, though there may be immature males within the group – and their communication will be conditioned by the needs of that situation. When that herd of horses is gathered off the mountain and confined within a field its behaviour pattern is broken. The horses' freedom of movement has gone, which means that the signs concerned with that movement will no longer be used; and they will be in much closer proximity to each other and so certain signs and sounds will be used less and others will be used more. When they have been broken and handled by men the variation in the signs and sounds used will be even more marked, especially if the horses are permanently stabled. Some signals, such as those of alarm and those of movement, will almost never be used, and others such as those signalling impatience or demand for food will have to be evolved by the horses themselves, either through imitating other horses or out of their own ingenuity. Since the horse has only eleven different tones of voice and is unable to create new tones to convey new messages, this means that he has to adapt and duplicate his existing vocal messages to meet his new needs. Whilst he will be able to adapt a large number of his existing signs, he will also need to invent a number of new signs, and this he will do either by imitating a sign used by another animal (usually, but not necessarily, another horse), or he will find that a sign he uses at random gets a particular response and he will then use that sign again to gain that response.

One of the experiments we used to show how a horse extends its vocabulary is very simple to reproduce. We would take a wild pony from the mountains and put him or her with my wife's hunter, then, when it was feeding time, old Cork Beg would whinney for food, and within a very short time his companion would be whinneying in imitation. When segregated the young horse would still ask for food when hungry, but not necessarily in the same way as Cork Beg. Of some one hundred and twenty-two observed cases, only three had not learnt to ask for food within seven days of contact with horses who were already asking for food. We found that there are four basically different ways of doing this and it is unlikely that any two horses within a small group will ask for food in precisely the same way, but in each case there will be little doubt as to what he is saying, and he will be easily understood. Since we found it almost impossible to differentiate between those sounds learned from association with man and other domesticated horses, and those messages which are natural to the horse, we decided in our dictionary of horse messages, which we were then beginning to compile, to list the meanings of all signs and sounds used, as they are all intended to convey a meaning and can be understood by other horses and by man. The distinction between 'natural' language and language learnt in domestication is further obscured by the fact that some sounds may be used comparatively rarely in the wild, then after contact with human beings and domesticated horses become common. One example is the message of welcome. In the wild the horse will stay in a reasonably settled herd, and a horse returning to the herd is greeted by gentle blowing through the nostrils, or a low whicker, or a nuzzle, all of which mean 'welcome'. The same phrase will be used by a mare calling her foal to her, by a mare reassuring her foal, and occasionally by other horses in the herd greeting each other, but it is not in common use. As a result of contact with man, it becomes very commonly used. When I pass my horses, I talk to them, I say 'hello' and they greet me in return. Some will blow through their nostrils, some will nuzzle me, some will give me the whicker of welcome, and my mare Iantella will kiss me. They will use the same phrases also when I feed them, and they will greet their friends on return to the stable with the same whicker of welcome.

To anyone interested in academic research, it is crucial to discover whether a particular sign or sound is natural to an animal in the wild, or merely acquired from association with man. But to the practical horseman who only wants to understand his horse, the distinction between natural and acquired language is unimportant.

4: *How a Horse Uses Sound*

One of the early difficulties we discovered in studying the sounds made by a horse and trying to make sense of them, is that unlike man a horse uses no set sequence of sounds to convey any meaning. In compiling our dictionary we very quickly found that, apart from a few exceptions, it is impossible to say that a certain sound means a certain thing, but it is possible to say that within certain limits a horse will convey a particular message in one of a number of ways. To try and understand this, we had another look at the human languages, and we realised that to convey a certain meaning the human being might use a thousand different sounds, but you could not be certain that any particular sound used by a human being would mean a definite thing. This may sound complete nonsense at first sight, but if you look at it you will see that it is so. The human species is made up of a myriad different nations, and each nation has its own language and dialects. If you take a common phrase like 'I love you,' each race, each nation and each tribe will have a different set of sounds in common use to convey this one phrase. Even within a single language, such as English, there are different ways of saying 'I love you.'

So in our dictionary of horse phrases, we have set out each message in English, and against it listed every individual way we know of that a horse uses to convey that message. We have taken for instance the simple phrase 'I love you,' using it as a broad way of denoting all signs of affection, and against that we have listed the various ways in which the horse denotes affection. We start with breathing out with two imperatives, breathing in with two imperatives, the whicker of welcome with three imperatives. These are the vocal ways

53

by which the horse shows affection. Then there are in addition a very large number of signs, and we have found twenty-six variations of these. That is to say that we conclude that most horses will show affection in one of twenty-six various ways. You will of course get an odd individual who will be outside the mainstream and show affection in a very odd way : for example Fearless denoted affection, when I came back from overseas, by galloping up with her ears flat back, skidding to a halt and licking me all over, then picking me up in her teeth and shaking me. We had another case of a Welsh pony stallion who had been recently castrated and who had been running with cattle, who denoted affection for a mare by smelling her urine as she made water. There are also one or two signs of attraction in sex play, but we do not include those with the phrase 'I love you' as they really mean something completely different. The girlish giggle of the mare when she squeals, and the stallion's whistle, are both sexual in impulse, not affectionate, for it is unusual for anything except sexual attraction to be involved in the mating of horses.

In effect, then, we have compiled an English-Horse dictionary. In it we have taken each of forty-seven phrases used by the horse, together with fifty-four sub-messages, and we have noted the various ways in which most horses will convey each meaning. This method is the opposite to that of most other people working in this field, who have tried to allocate a meaning to each sign or sound. This approach seems to us merely to increase the difficulties. But to make a dictionary of the more common phrases and messages used by a horse is a comparatively easy task. First you select a horse that you know well and are handling daily, and use him as the primary object of your study. You list the phrases, that is the signs and sounds, he uses that you understand. Some of these will be conveyed by signs alone, some by sound, but most by a mixture of signs and sounds. You will be surprised to find how many you already understand. This will probably be about half of what he is saying, and then by observation you will try to interpret the other phrases and sentences he uses. Since you will already know about half of what he is saying, these other signs and sounds will be comparatively easy to put a meaning to. After anything from six weeks to a year, you will find that you have got a list of between twenty-five and thirty-five basic messages that your horse frequently uses. Then, when you can understand everything your horse is saying, you can start observing other horses, and against the basic messages that you have listed for your own horse, you can list the ways that other horses have of saying the same thing. You will find that some of the horses will use phrases your own horse, that is your primary subject, used, and some will convey messages that your primary subject did not even attempt, and this will add to your list of common phrases.

In time – anything up to about twenty years! – you will perhaps have all the forty-seven basic messages used by the horse. Some of these, such as the scream of rage or terror, you may never hear, others which are confined to set situations such as lovemaking, or mothering of a foal, you will not often come across unless you keep breeding stock. So your list of basic messages may be less than my total of forty-seven basic messages and fifty-four sub-messages, but you will still have a list of all the messages used by the horses you come into contact with, and this can be added to from time to time. You will find that with some messages there are very few variations in the number of ways a horse will express himself, but for others you will find up to thirty variations, and the list is never complete. There is always one particular horse who will say something in a way you have not come across before.

As one example of the range of variations, the phrase 'where is my bloody breakfast' can be said by a horse in sound alone, by using the basic phrase 'welcome', and its six imperatives: that is, two degrees of blowing through the nostrils, a low whicker, a high whicker, a low whinney and a high whinney. A horse may also use a snort or even a neigh. Then there are a dozen or so signs or combinations of signs and sounds.

The fact that the phrase 'welcome' can also be used to mean 'where is my bloody breakfast' highlights the difficulty in getting any sense out of any set sequence of notes. The whicker of welcome which is used by a horse when he is greeting another, can become at feeding time 'where is my bloody breakfast.' Equally the mare can use the same set of notes to call her foal to her, or a stallion and mare can use it as a prelude to love play. The same sound can mean a number of things, depending on the circumstances in which it is used.

Old Cork Beg, for instance, uses the same call to say 'hello' to my wife or another horse, to say 'good, here is breakfast,' to me, or 'come here darling' to his current girl-friend. But this call can change to the imperative. If I am slow feeding him, or I feed another horse first, the notes he uses in his whicker of welcome quickly rise and the message becomes 'where is my bloody breakfast.' If his current girl-friend does not come when he calls her first, the note will rise and change from 'come here darling' to 'get over here you lazy little bitch.' The degree of imperative used depends in part on the personalities of the two horses concerned. Just as when my wife is handling the horses and says 'stop it,' it is a far stronger threat than if I say 'if you do that I'll have your guts for garters,' and the horses know it, so one horse might quite naturally use a much higher note of imperative to convey the same meaning than another. The increase or decrease in the imperative will be shown by raising or lower-ing the voice, as in human beings, as well as by adding to the original phrase or sentence. A man for example may increase the imperative by raising his voice in using the words 'come here,' or he may change the phrase from 'come here' to 'come here immediately.' The horse may increase the imperative by using a sign as well as increasing the volume of sound.

This approach to equine communication – instead of

putting our emphasis on the sound a horse makes, such as most researchers have done, we have put the emphasis on the meaning conveyed by *sounds and signs as a whole* – has been our major breakthrough and is I think our major contribution to the understanding of animal communication.

The volume and pitch of the voice is also determined by how far the horse is from the horse he is speaking to. For example when I am four or six hundred yards from home on one of my horses, he will shout at the top of his voice 'hello is anyone at home,' to which one of the horses in the stable will answer 'I am here.' The closer he gets to home, the lower he will have to pitch his voice to make himself heard, and the two horses will drop their voices the nearer they get to each other. When I get to the stable door they will still be saying the same thing, but instead of shouting at the top of their voices, they will just be blowing through their nostrils to each other. My horse will go on saying his welcome until he gets within sniffing distance of the other horse, and then he will stop saying welcome and use one of his calls to show affection. Now to anybody listening there is absolutely no difference in tone between the first call and the second call after he has been answered by another horse. A human parallel, perhaps, is in the words 'hello there'. If you go into the house of a friend, you might shout 'hello there,' to find out if there is anybody at home; he may answer you from upstairs, 'hello there,' and then when he comes downstairs you will greet each other quietly with the same word, 'hello'.

All these welcome calls could perhaps be translated by the world 'hello'. But we have not done so mainly because this would obscure the great variation in actual meaning. A mare welcoming her foal is conveying a very different message from the stallion trumpeting a challenge. The initial call of the stallion – 'is there anybody about' – will change very little in sound when it is answered, but the meaning of his call will change to 'come and fight,' if answered by another stallion, and will then go on to increasing provocation until they meet. But if he is answered by a mare he will go on calling the same call, but in this case 'is there anybody about' changes to 'come and make love,' and he will go on using this until he gets closer to her, when the imperative will drop to welcome, and she will either snap and kick at him, telling him to find another fancy piece, or she will give a girlish giggle and they will start their love play. And if a gelding answers, the stallion will tell him to bugger off in no uncertain terms. In every case the stallion's call will sound much the same, but the message will be completely different. The voice of the horse is only a guide to the meaning of the message, it does not convey the message itself, as the speech of a human being does.

It is of course also possible for a human being to make himself understood by someone who speaks a different language, simply by the use of signs and the tone of his voice. If you do not believe this you only have to observe any sailor landing in a foreign port. In a very short time he will have made his needs known and had his requirements fulfilled – usually booze, women and entertainment in that order – and he will not need a word of the language to make himself understood.

With horses, the context of the call gives you the meaning. This is why the work done on tape-recordings of horse calls has been so difficult to understand – no tape-recording can give you the context of the signal. Of course it is possible to misinterpret calls – I have seen a horse misinterpret the call of another horse. My wife's Welsh Cob Rostellan once answered the call of a stallion I had recently purchased and had castrated. When he was turned out for the first time, the stallion trotted into the field and called 'is there anybody about?' and Rostellan answered. They proceeded to call to each other until they were within sight of each other, then Rostellan trotted over to the stallion thinking he was saying 'welcome,' and got kicked in the ribs for his pains.

Since as well as understanding what your horse is saying, you want him to understand what you are saying, it is vital that you use your voice correctly in speaking to him. Unless you are an animal imitator by profession, it is of no use whatever to try to use the notes and tones that he uses, other than those in the lower ranges – that is, breathing in softly and breathing out softly. You can also get a very low whicker from your own vocal range. But further than this, it is pointless to try to imitate another horse, and in any case the horse will soon be able to interpret your own normal tones. Most of the rider's verbal control of his horse depends on simple commands in English, such as 'whoa', 'walk on', 'trot on', and the horse will learn to respond to these extremely quickly provided you use a correct method of training. When the horse responds to the word of command, he should be praised and caressed. He should be taught by encouragement, not punishment. For if you say 'whoa' and he moves on and you catch him a clout, he will very quickly associate 'whoa' with being hit and will never learn the word of command. Certain commands will in any case get an automatic response from a very high percentage of the horses you handle, and 'whoa' is one of them. About seventy percent of horses who have never been handled, will respond naturally to the word 'whoa'. Similarly, if you click your tongue the horse will go forward and become excited. If you say 'stand up', the horse will draw himself together naturally. These sounds seem to produce an automatic response in the horse, and should not be confused with commands that have to be taught him.

Of course when you are commanding your horse, the tone of the voice is extremely important. I have already referred to the Irishman, Dan Sullivan, who was known as the Whisperer. If you whisper to your horse very softly, he will find that the tone caresses him and it has almost exactly the same effect as caressing him with your hand. If you talk to him in a singsong gentle voice (I usually recite a little verse, 'there's a clever boy, there's a clever boy, there's a clever little fellow'), you will find it automatically steadies the horse and settles him if he is excited. If you speak to him in a sharp voice he will draw himself together and become alert. If you shout at him he knows you are angry. All these tones of the voice and those in between will draw an automatic response.

But you have to be extremely careful how you use them. Four or five years ago I had a very brilliant sheepdog who had the makings of a champion, but she was so keen and so enthusiastic that she was not very obedient to command. After some three months of training, unless I shouted at her and said 'Damn you Fan' before I gave the command, she would go on with what she was doing. And this was simply because when she was extremely disobedient, I used to curse her by saying 'Damn you Fan', and throwing a pebble in her direction so that she would know that she had to do what I told her to. So after this all my commands had to be prefaced with 'Damn you Fan'.

The horse is of course extremely responsive to the voice. On one occasion I was hauling cowdung with Fearless and a young cart colt which we were breaking, up into a very steep field. The cart colt was in the shafts and Fearless was in the trace harness. To get up into the field you used to have to take it as fast as you could, which meant the horses were cantering and you were running beside the horse in the shafts, and on this particular occasion, just as we got into the gateway, I slipped and my leg went under the cart and the colt's hind legs. I shouted 'Whoa Fearless' in a desperate voice, and Fearless stopped immediately and kicked the cart colt in the face, so that he stopped and threw himself back into the breeching. The wheel had stopped just on my leg, you could see the mark of the wheel on my thigh, but if it had gone over me, with ten or fifteen hundred weight of dung in the cart, I would never have walked again. This is a perfect example of the way a horse will respond to the tone of your voice. If I had said 'Whoa Fearless' in a normal tone, it would have been an even chance that she would have taken no notice of me whatever, but on this occasion she stopped instantly and stopped the colt as well. That was one of the reasons I had a very great affection for the old cow.

My father had a theory that when you were breaking a young horse it was very important to throw him on to the ground and teach him to lie down when you told him to. He used to throw the horse, and once it was down, sit on top of it and smoke his pipe or a burma cheroot, which he was very partial to, and recite marathon verses: usually 'The Man from the Snowy River' or 'Kissing Cups Race'. By the time he had recited those two, he used to swear that any horse would be quiet, and usually it was. This was in fact an extreme test of obedience, because anything that could stay within half a mile of the boss when he was smoking one of his burma cheroots at full steam must have been under remarkable control. But the principle of reciting verses is an extremely sound one, for we have found repeatedly with the untouched horses that we get here that reciting or singing to them anything that is soothing and rather monotonous, will settle and relax them, and, which is probably just as important, make you relaxed. For if you are close to the horse your emotions and feelings will be reflected by him; if you are nervous, he will be nervous, and if you are relaxed and speaking in a relaxed way, he will be relaxed as well.

5: *How a Horse uses Signs*

In the preceding two chapters I have tried to show how the horse uses his voice to convey a meaning. But it must be obvious to anyone who has observed horses that a horse also uses signs in various ways: to convey an intention, to draw attention to an object, as a warning, and sometimes to express an opinion. He will tend to look to the left if he is going to turn to the left and he will look to the right if he wants to turn to the right – that is the way he tells you which way he is going to go. He will raise his head and prick his ears and look intently at an object to draw your attention to it. He will put his ears back and raise his hind leg to warn you that if you come any nearer he will kick. If you give him something to eat which he does not like, he will take a mouthful and spit it out again, thus telling you what he thinks of it.

The use of sign language is of course not just confined to horses. All animals, including human beings, use signs as an integral part of their communication with other members of the species. We get the meaning of a conversation as much from the expression on the face and the use of the hands as we do from the tone of voice. The words 'I hate you and I am going to make you suffer,' used in one context are threatening and aggressive, but used by a man who is kissing and caressing a woman they mean a different thing altogether. I have already described how Cork Beg, when he uses the welcome tone, can mean 'welcome', 'good, here is breakfast' or 'come here' depending on whether he is nibbling my wife's coat, pushing his food basin around, or calling his girlfriend in the field. Equally, if a mare puts her ears back, squeals and raises her foot to kick, she is saying 'if you do not go away I will kick your teeth in.' But if on the other hand she squeals, kicks and raises her tail when a stallion is around, she is horseing and it means a different thing altogether. We call this her girlish giggle. So you can see that with the addition of a different sign, the same vocal note can mean two totally different messages: in fact two diametrically opposite messages, 'go away' and 'come and make love.'

The sign language is in fact much more easily understood than the vocal parts of the message, and it has always been a mystery to me why, with the exception of Meech and Ewbank in their work on pigs at Liverpool University, and one or two others, the modern researcher has not concentrated more on the sign language in work on animal communication. With horses at least, signs are of a much more regular pattern than sounds, and the intention of the horse is easily interpreted from the signs he uses. Added to this is the fact that sign language is similar in all breeds, ages and sexes of horses, though there are one or two exceptions, such as sexual sounds, and those limited to use by a foal calling 'I am only small.' The foal says this last when he is approaching a bigger horse that he is not sure about, by putting his head down as if he is going to suckle a mare, opening his mouth slightly, curving his lips back and making sucking motions with his tongue. He does this because he knows a bigger horse will then realize he is a foal and not kick or bite him. This is a sign common to very nearly all foals, though you get it also in some yearlings, and I have seen it done once by a four-year-old gelding. Sign language is almost universal among human beings too, and is the same irrespective of what race a man belongs to.

It is of course almost impossible to give a definite meaning to any movement taken in isolation. For example, if a horse waves a hind leg, he may mean 'I am going to kick,' or he may mean 'my foot hurts.' The vigour of the movement, the situation in which it is made, and the sounds made before and after all go to indicate meaning. Anyone who knows the horse well will be able to interpret the meaning of the signs very easily indeed.

There are between seventy and eighty different signs used by a horse. These depend on the age of the horse, and whether it is a stallion, mare or gelding. All these signs are used as part of the forty-seven basic messages and fifty-four sub-messages, and are usually used in conjunction with sounds, though there are certain cases when the message is conveyed solely by signs, especially when the horse uses only his head and ears. When a horse is conveying a message by signs he uses his muzzle, nose, mouth, eyes, ears, the whole head and neck, his skin, his tail, his legs and his feet. The legs and feet can be used either singly or as a pair: that is, the front legs may be used singly or as a pair, and so may the hind legs. A horse in the wild will normally use his hind legs only as a defensive weapon, and his front legs and teeth as an offensive weapon, though it is very little consolation to someone lying in hospital with a broken leg to know that the horse was only defending himself.

The unusual thing about sign language is that you sometimes come across very odd signs indeed, often acquired by the horse from other animals. I have already mentioned our eleven-two Welsh pony who had not been much in contact with other horses most of the year, and had been running with a herd of cattle, so when a mare made water, he would put his nose under it and sniff at it in exactly the same way a bull would sniff that of a cow. This is the only time I had come across this habit in a horse, and I have no doubt that he had acquired it from the cattle he had been running with.

Another pony we had cocked his leg like an immature dog, and when I traced this back, I found that the sheepdog on the farm he came from used to sleep in his stable. He and the pony were very great friends, and the pony had acquired the habit of cocking his leg by imitation of the dog. But funnily enough he would do it only over a spot where a mare had made water and not where a gelding had done so.

In the horse's sign language the head and neck are of course the most used parts of the body. They may be used as a whole to convey a message, or the various part may be used separately. The muzzle and the lips are used mainly to indicate affection – to caress and reassure a foal or another horse, and in love play – though they may also be used to investigate something and to draw attention to a special object. When a horse nuzzles you or when he nuzzles another horse, he is using his nose to show affection for you. When a foal is frightened it will run to its mother and she will nuzzle the foal to reassure it. In effect one horse nuzzling another is using its nose as an extension of the welcome sign, but when a mare nuzzles her foal to reassure it, she is saying, 'all right, mummy's here.'

Most people, when they are bitten by a horse, know only that it hurts and that they do not like it. But in actual fact there are four completely different sorts of bites from a horse. In love play, the mouth, teeth and lips are used a great deal and all four different types of bite may be used. A stallion will approach a mare and nip her. The mare will then swing her head round and snap at the horse, and the way she uses her head and neck is an indication of how she is receiving the stallion's attention. She may just swing her head round and nip him affectionately, or she may swing her head and snap at him, telling him to go away. She may even punch him with her teeth, or bring her head round and fasten her teeth in his skin, really biting him in rejection. If his intentions are received in any sort of encouraging manner, the stallion will nip and caress the mare's flanks and loins with his lips, and very often he will grip the mare's neck with his teeth, without actually biting her. Thus in a single sequence the stallion has nipped the mare as a token of affection and gripped her in his teeth to indicate his passion. The mare in return has either nipped the stallion with affection, snapped at him or punched him with her teeth, or in an extreme case really caught hold of him in anger.

Each of these four gestures means something completely different. When the mare nipped him, she said 'darling stop it' and when she snapped at him, she said 'go away and leave me alone.' Then she either punched him with her teeth or really bit him. The punch with the teeth is more commonly seen. The teeth and head are brought forward in a lunging or swinging movement and the teeth hit the other horse. They are not closed and it is a blow not a bite, though it is often confused with the bite, which is a similar movement of the head and neck, though the teeth in this case are closed on the opponent. If they are promptly opened again, this is a snap. But the horse may hold on, closing his teeth with all his power, though this is very rarely seen, and is used normally only in the wild by two stallions fighting. The punch on the other hand is often seen, most commonly as a warning, though if the warning is not heeded, the horse will go on to snap or bite. It is generally wise to heed the warning, for if a horse really catches hold of you, you will be hurt. If he catches hold of your arm, he will probably break it. If he catches hold of your shoulder, he will pick you up and shake you, (though this is most uncommon, and you must only hope that it never happens to you).

Unlike the eyes of a human being, which speak a language of their own, the eyes of a horse change expression very little. They are used only to indicate what the horse is looking at. But the ears on the other hand, which are scarcely used in the sign language of humans, have an infinite variety of meanings to express. They are used not only separately, but also with other parts of the body, to convey an intention, to draw attention to an object or an incident, and above all to convey the mood of the horse. Most people know that when a horse lays his ears flat back as far as they will go, he is hostile, and he is warning you to keep away. When the ears are half-way between the upright and back position, it usually means that he is relaxed and doing nothing, and not worried about anything. But if the ears are set in this position, and not just lying there anyhow, it means that he is looking at you behind him, and possibly listening to what you are saying to him. When I am riding and handling a horse I talk to him a great deal of the time, and the horse keeps his ears half-back, just listening to the tone of my voice. I always say that he is listening for my words of wisdom, but in actual fact he is only listening to the tone of my voice. A horse also points his ears sideways, to one side or the other to draw attention to an object. He will look at an object and appear to be listening to it at the same time, probably listening to hear if the object is making a hostile sound, at the same time as he is looking for a hostile movement. When a horse has his ears three-quarters pricked it means 'I am awake and alert, let's go,' and when the ears are fully pricked it means that the horse is drawing attention to or looking at an object. But when the ears are stiffly pointing sideways it is a sure indication that the horse is going to have a go at you. Like the ears laid back, this position means that the horse is hostile. But whereas when the ears are flat back the rest of the body may be half or three-quarters relaxed, when the ears are pointing sideways every muscle of the body will be taut as well. He may be going to buck, kick or rear or have a go at you with his teeth. The ears can be used as a guide to the horse's mood in nine hundred and ninety-nine cases out of a thousand.

We did have a horse some years ago, a registered Welsh Cob, who was just plain mentally unbalanced. No matter what he was going to do, he always had his ears sweetly pricked as if he were a kind and gentle horse. But this horse was the worst horse I have ever handled. I have seen him buck, rear, roll, throw himself over backwards, spin round bucking, spin round rearing, try to knock you off against a tree, try to crush you against a wall, kick, and strike out with his front feet. Yet he would do all of these things as if he were going as sweetly and kindly as a baby. Three or four people had tried to break him, two of them very cruelly and the third had made him completely hostile to human beings. Though after having him for about three months I could do anything with him, he was still dangerous to any other human being. Horses will very often buck for pleasure and they will enjoy doing so, particularly when their owners themselves enjoy their horses bucking, and in this case the horse will very often buck with his ears pricked. But here the buck is *joie de vivre* and there is no intent to get you off. Old Cork Beg used to buck with my wife until he got her laughing, as I have already described.

The head and neck when used together to make a sign are used to draw attention to an object, or to convey an intention of going in a certain direction. When the neck and teeth are used either to bite or punch, they are used to make a threat against another horse. The legs, teeth and tail of course are generally used to convey a warning of hostile intent; but it must always be remembered that the raising of the foot can mean 'my foot hurts', as well as 'I am going to kick you.' The difference between a warning and a definite threat is usually conveyed by the vigour of the movement, but this varies from horse to horse, as does the degree of violence of language among human beings. One horse may lift his leg and wave it and mean absolutely nothing, the second horse doing exactly the same thing may be making a very real and definite threat, and you may get a third horse which will raise his foot only a couple of inches from the ground as a warning. If you do not pay attention the next thing you know is that you will be picking your teeth out of the gutter. The vigour of the movement in the horse or the strength of the language in the human being are an individual thing and you must know the individual before you can gauge the strength of the message.

The skin of the horse also speaks. It is usually used to convey a response; for example, if you touch a sore part of the body and the horse twitches his skin and flinches, he is saying 'that hurts.' On occasion horses will twitch their skin spontaneously to tell you that that part of the body is sore. The muscles will indicate the mood of the horse, whether they are taut or relaxed. According to which muscles are being tightened or relaxed, they will also convey to you exactly which part of the horse is going to react next. For example, if the back muscles are tightened it shows you the horse is going to buck. And the tail is used to convey hostile intent; or to indicate sexual response (in a mare). Or if it is held up and out it simply shows that the horse is alert and awake – in effect the the horse will use its tail to say 'let's go'. The tail tends to be used in conjunction with the head and neck – if the head is raised, the tail will be, if the neck is relaxed the tail will rest into the buttocks.

It must also be remembered that all these signs can be, and very often are, used with the vocal part of a message. This may only be a sharp intake of the breath or a blowing through the nostrils, or it may be a squeal of rage. Unlike the vocal range of the messages, the number of signs varies very little from horse to horse, but combined with the voice and e.s.p. the number of messages conveyed by signs varies considerably.

One of the most emotional moments of my life happened whilst I was in the Army. I had just come back from overseas, and when I came home the first thing I did was to go out and see the horses. They were all grazing at the far end of a ten-acre field, which was about six hundred yards long. I stood at the gate and shouted 'come on my darlings'. They all looked up and came flat-out up the field, led by Fearless. She was galloping as fast as she could with her head stuck out and her ears flat back and her mouth open. Even after eight years she was still liable to have a piece out of you or to clout you with her front feet, and since I had gone too far down the field to make a run for it, I stood still. When she got to within ten yards of me she stuck her four feet into the ground and skidded to a stop. Then she took two steps forward and licked me all over from head to foot, and when she had done this for about three minutes the tears were running down my cheeks, so she thought that was enough of a good thing. Just to show me the status was still quo, she caught hold of me with her teeth and lifted me from the ground and shook me slowly backward and forwards four or five times, then she put me down, and rubbed me with her nose. I have never been so touched in all my life, the display of affection was somewhat unusual in form, but it was fantastic.

Another example of unorthodox display of affection befell a friend of mine. I sold him a very nice quiet gentle mare. He did not know a lot about horses, but he and the mare got on extremely well for a long time, until one day I had a desperate telephone call from him. The mare was in pain and would I go over. So I went straight out to his place and asked him what was the matter. He said 'Oh she seems all right, until I go into her stall, and as soon as I go in and touch her, she squeals and waves her hind leg and makes water.' Then he took me out and showed me. As soon as I got there I saw what had happened. It was merely that the mare was horse-ing. She had fallen in love with her new owner as if he were a stallion, and she was showing her affection the only way she knew.

6: *Our Dictionary of Horse Language*

I have been referring to messages, sub-messages and variations. These terms of course are rather vague and indefinite. This is because animal communication itself is very indefinite since the interpretation of any message is a personal matter. A message as we define it is an intention, a threat or an enquiry, a feeling or a statement made by a horse. A sub-message is a response to or a development of a message. The term 'variation' is an abbreviation of the self-explanatory phrase, 'variation from the most common way of conveying a message or a sub-message'. Some messages can be conveyed in a number of different ways, by signs, sounds and various combinations of the two. In our observation of some three hundred horses, we have noted thirty different ways of saying 'welcome', and also about thirty variations on 'where is my breakfast.' But the foal's 'I am only small' is said in only two or three ways, and most messages have six to ten variations.

In our dictionary of signs and sounds we have not listed most of these, but for the purpose of this book we have abbreviated the list to the most common ways of saying each phrase. The phrases we have used to convey any particular message have just happened, there is no particular thought behind them, though of course we have tried to convey the feeling of the message by the words and phrases we have used. You will see in the dictionary that some similar messages will be described by two or three different phrases, but you will also see that the context of the message is different and therefore the message itself is different. This applies particularly to messages that are almost sub-messages in that they are developments of an original statement, but since they are at times used alone, we have listed them under messages. Anyone who is interested in equine communication will in any case need to compile his own dictionary and will of course use his own words to describe each message – he may decide to dispense with the distinction we have made between messages and sub-messages; or include some imperatives or some variations as separate messages. Since each horse will convey his oral and visual messages differently, so each person's dictionary will be laid out differently. But as a guide to anyone who wants to understand his or her own horse I am including a very abbreviated form of my own dictionary. I have made first an alphabetical list of English phrases, noting the number of sub-messages attached to each phrase, and a reference by number to the full translation set out below. Thus, if you want to know how a horse communicates the idea 'I love you' and its two sub-messages, you turn to number 16 below.

Phrase	Number of sub-messages	Reference number of message
Come and drink	I	24
Come and fight	4	18
Come and get it	–	20
Come here	I	5
Come on	3	11
Come on then	–	37
Don't do that	2	25
Don't go away	2	6
Don't leave me behind	–	38
Don't worry	–	32
Gangway	I	34
Go away	2	12
Help	–	30
I am boss	I	33
I am enjoying this	–	39
I am frightened	–	28
I am here	–	9
I am hungry	3	36
I am king	–	19

Phrase	Number of sub-messages	Reference number of message
I am only small	—	27
I am thirsty	—	26
I am tired	1	41
I cannot	1	42
I hate you	2	17
I love you	2	16
I suppose I will have to	—	43
I will buck	—	44
Is anybody about?	—	7
It is good to be free	—	47
Let us get the hell out of here	—	29
Let us go	1	40
Look	4	4
Mummy loves you	1	23
Oh my God	—	31
Scratch here	—	46
Stop it	2	13
That hurts	1	14
That is nice	—	15
That tickles	—	45
There you are	—	10
We are good girls here	5	22
Welcome	—	1
What's this?	2	3
Where are you?	—	8
Where is my bloody breakfast?	6	35
Who are you?	2	2
You will be quite safe with me	4	21

1. *Welcome.* This is used to generalize all calls and signs of greeting used between horses, the most common of which is the whicker of welcome. The strength of the call and the vigour of the movement indicate the degree of imperative. The context, and the carriage of the head and tail, indicate the purpose of the welcome.

2. *Who are you?* is used by two strange horses on meeting. It is an extension of the 'welcome' phrase and is said by sniffing or more usually blowing at each other. The attitude of the two horses towards each other is indicated by the harshness or the gentleness of the blowing and the carriage of the head and tail. This procedure leads to the sub-messages, (1) *I am a friend,* said by continuation of the gentle blowing and other friendly movements, or (2) *go to hell,* a snap or nip by one or other horse, a stamp on the ground with a front foot, a threat to kick, or a squeal.

3. *What's this?* is used in reference to objects which are close at hand, usually said by a sniff at the object; but a horse may paw the object with his front foot. This gesture leads to the sub-messages, (1) *it's all right,* shown by approaching and inspecting and then ignoring strange objects, or (2) *it's dangerous,* shown by moving away, by shying at the object or attacking the danger.

4. *Look,* used to draw attention to an object and denoted by raising the head and tail and snorting or whinneying to attract the attention of other horses. Similar, and a sub-message to 'look', is (1) *what is that,* which is said by raising the head high and pricking the ears and looking at a strange object. There is no sound as a secondary reaction to 'what is that'. The horses will either respond *it is all right* or *it is dangerous.* Another sub-message is (2) *let's go this way.* The horse says this by looking in the direction he wants to go and moving in that direction. A second horse responding to 'what is that' will look at the object, and if he recognizes it will say (3) *nothing to bother about,* or (4) *look out,* using a snort or a neigh of warning.

5. *Come here.* This starts as a whicker of welcome rising in the imperative, which may also be shown by shaking the head back and forwards if there is no response. The message may be changed to *if you do not come here, I will have your guts for garters,* which is shown by a threatening movement and will draw the response, (1) *all right I am coming,* usually said by a low whicker.

6. *Don't go away.* This is a whicker or whinney to call a companion back, and varies from a whicker of welcome to the 'where are you' neigh. This is often used also for the sub-messages, (1) *where are you going?*, or (2) *wait for me.*

7. *Is anybody about?* A loud neigh repeated several times. This has an enquiring note and is used with the head and tail held high. When it is answered – with another loud neigh meaning 'I am here' – the first horse will then use the following message :

8. *Where are you?* 'Where are you' may thus be a sub-message of 'is anybody about?' When it is used by a mare looking for her foal, or by a horse looking for a friend. 'Where are you?' will be a whinney rather than a neigh.

9. *I am here!* is a loud neigh used in answer to 'is anybody about?' This will be repeated until the two horses are in sight of each other. This again my be used as a sub-message as in the sequence described in 7 and 8 above.

10. *There you are.* This is used at a distance in answer to 'where are you?', and is usually a whinney as the two horses approach each other, which will change to a whicker of welcome as they meet.

11. *Come on!* This is used when two horses are grazing together or resting, and one wants to move away or play. He will indicate this by nudging his companion or dancing round him and nipping him. He may give a whicker or just walk away hoping his companion will follow. He may get the responses (1) *oh all right*, shown in the reluctant carriage of his companion; or (2) *yes let's* – an enthusiastic response – or (3) *I'm damned if I will!*, shown simply by a negative response or even by threatening or snapping.

12. *Go away!* This is a defensive sign and is designed purely to protect. It can be a mild threat, usually made with the teeth or hind legs, possibly only one hind leg. If this is ignored the stronger warning *go away or I will clobber you* follows. This is a definite and hostile movement and quickly becomes *you have asked for it*, which is an attempt to bite or kick the tormentor.

13. *Stop it!* This is a response to an action by another horse or a human. It varies from twitching the skin to striking with the front leg, kicking or biting. This has a response (1) *sorry*, shown by a rapid evacuation of the area with an air of injured innocence or (2) *I will if I want to*, which is shown by intensification of the annoying action.

14. *That hurts.* This is shown by flinching or twitching the skin and shying away from the aggressor. It has a sub-message (1) *my foot hurts*, shown by lifting up the foot and limping. Variations include *my back hurts, my neck hurts, my head hurts*, or anything else, but we have counted this as one sub-message.

15. *That is nice!* is a response to any action that is pleasing to the horse and it appears three times in sub-messages, but it is used as a message in its own right and as a plea to continue. It is shown by an increase of pressure on the partner and is used when two horses are in close contact, maybe accompanied by a grunt of contentment or by breathing out.

16. *I love you.* We use this phrase to show affection other than maternal or sexual. There are thirty or more ways of showing this, the most common being a gentle blowing through the nostrils or rubbing with the nose and head. This can draw the response, (1) *I love you too*, or (2) *go away*.

17. *I hate you.* The signs and sounds used in this case are different from *go away*, and are of an aggressive rather than a defensive nature. The front legs and teeth will be used, which is a definite sign of antipathy between two horses, and if it draws the response (1) *I hate you too*, a fight will ensue. It may draw the response (2) *I am sorry*, as in message 13: the same sorry signs will be used, but they will also include the defensive actions, that is the hind quarters will be presented or a pair of heels may be used on the aggressor.

18. *Come and fight.* This is a response to a stallion's challenge and is a high-pitched neigh, or perhaps a scream of rage. This is followed by (1) *I will pulverize you*, which is part of the preliminary manoeuvring and threatening to

try and establish a psychological advantage before fighting the battle. After the battle the loser will say (2) *I am sorry, I am going.* He does this by fleeing with his tail tucked in, and the winner in his triumph, threatens (3) *if you come back I will kill you.* The stallion will then go to his mares and say (4) *did you see that, girls, I murdered him.* He may do this by snorting and dancing round his mares, and he may also drive them away to safety. This cavorting signal of sheer triumph may also be used by a mare or gelding who has got the better of another horse or human being.

19. *I am king* is the bugle note of a stallion, which is either a challenge, or a call to a group of mares. This will be repeated again as he goes towards the mares.

20. *Come and get it.* This is the horseing mare's neigh in response to the stallion's bugle, and will be used as the horseing mare leaves the group to meet the stallion.

21. *You will be quite safe with me.* It is the first phrase of love play used by the stallion, and is said by blowing through his nostrils. Unless he gets a definite 'no' from the mare he will continue with this until he gets a girlish giggle, when he will say, (1) *I like you.* He does this by titillating the mare on her neck and flanks with his lips, and then (2), in a more urgent manner, he will say *let's make love* by nipping her with his teeth. Next he progresses to (3) *come on then*, which can be shown by gripping the neck with his teeth, by trying to mount her or by actually mounting the mare. The next sub-message will be (4) which is *that was good.* After he has served the mare he will dismount and arch his neck and nuzzle the mare, or he may snort, or otherwise show his affection.

22. *(Go away) we are good girls here.* This can be shown by a very aggressive action indeed towards the stallion. The lead will be taken by a very strong mare protecting the virtues of the rest of the herd from a rather immature stallion. This response may then change to (1) the girlish giggle, which is used in response to the stallion's 'you will be quite safe with me.' This is a squeal by the mare, and she may also wave her

hind leg, and may lead to (2) *what are we waiting for?* This is usually the phrase of a highly sexed mare, who will make water and stand with her hind legs open and her tail raised; or she may open and close her vuvula or stand with her vulvula slightly open. But mares are as unpredictable as women in their response to the male, and in her love play the mare can change very quickly from saying 'go away I am a good girl' to 'come and get it, what are you waiting for.' It all depends entirely on the mare. She may use all three messages as separate messages or start with 'go away' and use the other two as sub-messages. When the love-making is over she may say (3) *that was hard work.* She will say this by grunting, puffing and blowing and complaining thoroughly. She may say (4) *is that all?* by simply shaking herself and walking away to graze, or (5) she may say *that was nice, let's do it again.* Here she will whicker and try to initiate further love play.

These events, with any luck, will lead after eleven months to the birth of a foal the following spring, and the need for a further group of messages for use by the mare in the care of her foal. The first of these is:

23. *Mummy loves you.* The mare does this by nuzzling her foal and blowing gently through her nostrils. If her foal is frightened she will reassure it and say (1) *you will be quite safe.* She will do this by pushing the foal into her flank on the other side of danger.

24. *Come and drink.* She does this by a low whicker or whinney, moving one leg slightly sideways and offering the udder to the foal. If she does not want the foal to feed, she will say sub-message (1) *there is none there,* pushing the foal away with the upper part of her hind leg or her stifle joint or her nose. If the foal is naughty she will say:

25. *Don't do that.* This is different from the normal 'stop it' used between two horses, because 'stop it' will be said when two horses are in close proximity, and usually by signs. But the mare may warn her foal from a distance, usually in a sharp whinney while she threatens it with her head. This is followed by *mummy warned you!* raising the tone of voice

and increasing the vigour of movement. If the foal is still disobedient she will say, *right you have asked for it* and punish the foal, usually by nipping it. The foal itself will use a lot of the adult messages, but will have two of its own:

26. *I am thirsty.* This is shown by nuzzling the mare's flanks and trying to get to her udder.

When the foal is threatened by a bigger horse it will say:

27. *I am only small.* He says this by holding his head and neck out straight, sometimes holding the nose up slightly and moving the mouth as if sucking. When he does this it is most unlikely that another horse will hurt him.

28. *I am frightened.* This can be shown by a snort or a neigh, and if they are in a confined area the horses will lean against each other and gain reassurance from the group.

29. *Let us get the hell out of here*, is said with a snort or a neigh with the head and tail held high ready for flight, which in turn will draw a response of 'yes, let's', or 'nothing to worry about'.

30. *Help!* This is a scream of fear and is seldom heard. I have heard it only once but it is unmistakable.

31. *Oh my God!* This is a scream of pain and is only uttered by a horse suffering unbearable pain. Again it is quite unmistakable.

32. *Don't worry*, is used by a calm horse to steady a frightened one. It can be conveyed by a whicker, by offering protection to the other horse with the body or merely by reassuring bodily contact.

Another group of sounds is concerned with herd discipline. There is a definite social order within the herd, descending from the lead mare to the yearlings, small foals being usually disciplined by their mothers. Even in domestication this herd discipline will still be observed within a group. The senior member of the herd takes precedence in feeding, watering and moving, and may demand her rights with the threat:

33. *I am boss.* This is said to an inferior within the group,

usually by threatening with the head and teeth. The boss will also say *go back*, by swinging the head and threatening any inferior that tries to pass her. Next comes either *I will bite you* or *I will pulverize you* which involves driving the inferior away with her teeth and front legs. If the second horse is a social equal, it will respond to the statement 'I am boss', by saying (1) *no you are not*. This is expressed either by ignoring the threat altogether, or by threatening the other back. Similar messages are used in other situations — for example, *go back, I will kick* or *I will bite* may be used when the boss horse is feeding and an inferior horse approaches. In this case a threat to kick may be made.

34. *Gangway!* This is said by a boss horse by pushing through a herd and laying about the others with his head. On the other hand the sub-message (1) *Excuse me*, is used by an inferior horse trying to pass a boss horse.

There is another group of signs and sounds which have been developed by horses through their contact with man. Many of these deal with feeding. The first and possibly oldest of these is easily understood :

35. *Where is my bloody breakfast?* This is shown in a multitude of ways, from the whicker of welcome to a bang on the food bin. Each horse-owner will know how his horse does it. The sub-messages are several. (1) *I want water* is often expressed by knocking the water bowl about and whinneying. (2) *I want hay* may be said by walking to the hay rack looking disgusted. When he has been fed (3), the horse will say *thank you*, usually by using the whicker of welcome or saying *I love you* and showing affection. He will of course indicate whether or not he likes his food and will say (4) *this is nice*, by eating his food greedily with bits falling out of his mouth; or if you are feeding him tit-bits he will say (5) *give me some more*, by whickering and nuzzling at your pockets and nudging you to remind you he is still there. If he does not like what you give him he will say (6) *that is horrible* by spitting it out and wrinkling his lips and making ugly faces.

Whereas 'where is my bloody breakfast' is used by horses accustomed to being fed regularly, a horse which has never been fed will also say :

36. *I am hungry, or thirsty.* He will say this by whickering when he sees you, and putting on the appearance of being empty and miserable. Sub-message of this is (1) *I am wet,* which is very similar and said by standing in the rain with head down looking very miserable. If a horse has to go out into the rain he will say (2) *this is horrible* by turning his head away from the rain and going into it with reluctance and disgust. He can also say (3) *I am cold,* by shivering and again looking miserable.

When you are riding a horse there will be a continuous contact and interplay of messages. We will ignore the messages used by man to convey his wishes, as these are a matter of taste and training; and we have also dealt with a lot of the signs used by the horse already, because they are also used by horses between themselves; but they also use them in communicating with man. The first sign specific to riding, however, is :

37. *Come on then,* said by whickering and dancing round a little to show his desire to go out and enjoy himself. A companion left behind will shout :

38. *Do not leave me behind.* This is said with a neigh or a whinney and the horse may try to demolish the stable door in his anxiety to follow his companions. Once you have started your horse may be saying :

39. *I am enjoying this,* which he does by dancing about or walking along with his head and tail held high and generally showing his enjoyment. If he is feeling particularly well he will show his *joie de vivre* in an unmistakable way – *I feel fine* – by cavorting around and giving a little squeal or pretending to buck.

40. *Let us go!* is said by dancing around and reaching for his bit and showing a general desire to go faster. A sub-message to this is (1) *yes let's,* shown by an enthusiastic response to a request or an order to do something. After his work

he may be tired and he will say this too in an unmistakable way :

41. *I am tired*. He will communicate this by the way he carries himself. The sub-message is (1) *not again*, which he says by his reluctance to repeat an action. Of course not all horses are willing and keen, and at times they may refuse to do what they are asked to do and say :

42. *I cannot*, by refusing to do whatever it is. The sub-message (1) *I will not* differs from 'I cannot' only because you know quite well that he *can* do it. So if you can make him he may give in by saying :

43. *I suppose I will have to*, and he will show his reluctance in much the way that Shakespeare described the schoolboy 'creeping like snail unwillingly to school'. But before he capitulates he may well threaten :

44. *I will buck*. He points his ears sideways and arches his back and makes as if to buck. There are similar messages *I will rear*, said by throwing his head up and lifting his front feet off the ground, and *I will kick* or *I will bolt*.

45. *That tickles*, he says by twitching the skin and possibly waving a leg, stamping or squealing.

46. *Scratch here*, is shown by rubbing where the itch is. If he is with another horse, he will scratch the other horse with his teeth to show where he wants to be scratched.

Finally, here is the last message. When you turn a horse into the field he will say :

47. *It is good to be free!* And *joie de vivre* is something every horse expresses in his own individual way.

7: *E.S.P. and Weeping Roger*

Early in our researches we realized that the air and manner of the horse when he was delivering a message was all-important to interpreting what he was trying to say. But we quickly discovered also that there was more than this to the way we were receiving messages from our animals. It was not just the air and manner of delivery that was giving us the clues. There were also times when we knew instinctively the meaning of the message. And even when we could not see or hear the horse, we found that in times of stress or difficulty we could feel the uneasiness and know that something was wrong. Over and over again, when we went to see what was the matter, something was wrong.

Funnily enough the first time this happened after we had started on our research into animal communication, it was not a horse but a cow that was involved. Normally I sleep like a log and do not hear anything, but on this night I woke up with this powerful feeling that something was amiss, and went out to the animals. The cow was calving, but it was a breech delivery so she was in difficulties. Thinking about it afterwards, I worked out that I had been awakened by the feeling that something was wrong; and been drawn subconsciously to where the cow was. This started me thinking in a new direction and, step by step, I came to the somewhat startling conclusion that I could feel the moods of the horses rather than see or hear them. This faculty is what we call extra-sensory perception, perception outside the range of our normal five senses. And we realized that animals can use this faculty to convey moods, emotions and certain limited ideas. Since it is used in conjunction with other forms of communication – sounds and signs – it can be compared with the air and manner of delivery of speech in a human being; but it is more than this, because you *know* the mood and feel it within yourself. If a horse is excited, you feel it, and the horse will feel it when you are depressed and this is a matter of instinct rather than visual, aural or tactile perception.

This is the part of our work about which there is considerable controversy. I have been warned that entry into so highly contentious an area may tend to devalue our work on animal communication as a whole, in the eyes of the academic world. I have often been told that while our work on signs and sounds is far in advance of anything anybody else has done, our involvement with animal extra-sensory perception makes us suspect – even puts us in the same class as charlatans and music-hall acts! For scientists have been arguing for the past fifty years about whether extra-sensory perception exists or not: who are we to rush in where scholars fear to tread, and claim to have proved not only that it does exist, but that it exists among animals and is an integral part of their communication?

However, I must stand by my own view. The scepticism of some scientists does not of itself invalidate my conclusions. Until Faraday started his work with frogs and the single-cell battery, no doubt a section of the scientific world said that electricity did not exist, for any new field of research has been looked upon with suspicion by the scientific conservatives. We are absolutely convinced by our own experience that e.s.p. does exist, and we have proved, to our own satisfaction anyway, that it does. We know that we cannot have complete communication with horses without using e.s.p. We know that horses use it in communicating with each other. Therefore we must continue our researches into it, and I would be insincere if I did not deal with it in my account of the work we have done with horses. In fact, to carry out research into equine communication *without* taking into account e.s.p. and telepathy would be equivalent to trying to study English by studying only the nouns and verbs and pretending that adverbs and adjectives did not exist. Since our work is primary research and not secondary research, we have to study equine communication as a whole, not its parts. Subsequent researchers may, for example, be able to do more detailed studies on the use of sounds or signs or e.s.p. alone, but they will have the work we and other researchers have done into communication as a whole to give their detail a context.

A further area of argument about our work on e.s.p. with horses, even among those who do not totally reject the idea, has been around the degree of unconscious perception involved. When you are perceiving consciously, the argument runs, you can consciously see, hear and understand the signs and sounds made by a horse. But you also exercise a certain amount of unconscious perception: that is, without consciously knowing you are doing it, you see and hear certain things which help you understand the message which the horse is trying to convey. The charge is that we are confusing, to whatever extent, unconscious perception with extra-sensory perception. Now we have always realized that in a large number of cases this may be so, because when you are handling a horse, you do unconsciously observe and anticipate what he is going to do, and you do tend to put your understanding down to 'instinct'. Equally, no doubt, a herd of horses will realize unconsciously what you are feeling simply from your facial expression, your movement and the way you carry yourself. This is all unconscious perception, and we know that it is, but since it is not conscious we have, rightly or wrongly, included it under e.s.p., since we find it extremely difficult to set an exact border line between the unconscious and true e.s.p. There is of course room for considerable research here, and we may find when this has been done that we have mistaken a very large amount of unconscious perception for e.s.p. We are not really concerned at present – though we will be later – with whether unconscious perception is a fifth means of communication or not. Our research from the beginning has been very much a question of following a path to see where it goes. All the experimental work we have done on e.s.p. has in any case been designed in such a way that it can be duplicated at a later date

by other people in other places, so that our own work can be
verified, and anyone doing later research into equine communication has some standard experiments to carry out before
he goes on to experimental work of his own design. We hope
that this will be done time and time again, and that once
sufficient work has been done in the field of signs and sounds,
systematic experiments will be carried out on e.s.p.

We have done some experiments specifically on e.s.p., one
of which was a feeding experiment carried out between two
horses who had no visible or audible contact with each other;
but we cannot be absolutely certain that our horses' sense of
hearing does not allow them to pick up distant sounds unconsciously, and even less can we be certain that part of
equine communication is not the unconscious perception of
certain sounds that are normally considered to be inaudible.
We are led to believe by other scientific research that horses'
hearing is much the same as ours and that the horse does not
hear ultrasonic sounds : that is, previous scientific experiments
on horses have shown no reaction to ultrasonic sounds. On
the other hand it is quite possible that there are certain sounds
which are inaudible to us, which a horse will hear unconsciously, though we do not think that this is so. On the other
hand it is not without significance that in our experiments we
did not get any conclusive results except with what we call
empathic pairs.

The point is that any horse cannot communicate mentally
with any other horse, just as any human being cannot communicate mentally with any other human being. It is only if
you are very close to someone that you may be able to sense
what they are feeling without seeing them and talking to
them. When two horses are mentally and emotionally on the
same wavelength, then they too can sense what the other is
thinking and what the other is doing.

Now it is common practice for a horse handler, faced with
a very frightened or nervous horse, to use another horse that
is confident and relaxed to give the anxious one confidence

and relax him. We very often get sent a bunch of seven or eight three- and four-year-old cobs, horses and ponies which have never been handled and are completely wild, and we use one of two ways to get them settled and quiet. One is to approach the most settled cob in a quiet way and get him quiet, so that slowly the other horses in the bunch will become settled too, in tune with the horse we are handling. The second method, which we use more often, is to put the wild ponies in the stable together with one or two of our own horses. We leave them for half-an-hour to get accustomed to each other, then we go in to them. They will belt around the stable trying to get away from us, but our own horse will come over to talk, and we talk to him and feed him a few horse nuts, and we can then feel the others becoming gradually more relaxed. He will give them confidence in us and confidence in themselves.

Now it is obvious that the wild horses relax a certain amount from the example of the other horse. But we have found that we can do exactly the same thing with horses that are out of sight and sound of each other, *if the two horses are an empathic pair*, that is, if they are mentally in tune with each other. We can settle one horse by relaxing the other, or make one horse excited by exciting his companion.

This is one of our standard experiments. But it is in fact based on a trick as old as man's contact with horses. One of the earliest books on breaking horses for harness instructs you to take a colt and couple him to an old horse who will teach the young one to work. This method of horse-training has been used for hundreds of years. The South American *gauchos*, when they want to control a herd of horses, turn an old mare out with them and put a bell on her. The other horses will follow the old mare, and she will get them going quietly and steadily. The *gauchos* can then find the herd by the bell, and the old mare will make it possible to drive the young horses into a corral.

My early memories of seeing horses broken at home include

seeing Black Beauty, our pony, always in attendance 'as a schoolmaster' to tell the others what to do. Those were my father's words: he said that Beauty had to be there to tell the young horses what to do, and for some fifteen years we used Cork Beg for the same purpose. The older horse settles the younger horse and the young horse will imitate his senior. When a young horse is being asked to do something new his first reaction is to say 'I can't.' Seeing another horse do it will show him that it is not impossible, but seeing another horse can do it does not necessarily convince him that he can, so he may still say 'I can't.' However, if he can feel the other horse *enjoying* himself he will want to enjoy the experience too, and that is where extra-sensory perception comes in.

E.s.p. between animals is not a conscious mental process, it is an unconscious process and to a certain extent it is an automatic reflex. If an old hunter hears the sound of a hunting horn and hounds in full cry in the distance, he will become excited. This is because he associates the sound of the hunting horn and the cry of the hounds with being excited. But if he has a companion with him who has never heard hounds and does not know what a hunting horn means, the companion will become excited because the old horse is excited, without knowing why. The old horse's excitement is an automatic reflex and the young horse's excitement too is an automatic response. If you go into a stable and frighten a horse, his empathic companion, even though he may be out of sight and out of hearing, will also show signs of being frightened.

An empathic pair is simply a pair of horses mentally and emotionally close to each other, and the phenomenon comes about in one of two ways. Two horses may simply find themselves automatically in tune with each other from the first time they meet. These will probably be of the same breed and type. Or alternatively, they may become mentally in tune with each other through close and constant companionship. They will initially think roughly upon the same mental lines, but by close association they will attain complete empathy. If you get two thoroughbreds and turn them out with a herd of ponies, they will in most cases tends to graze together, probably away from the ponies, and in time they will become an empathic pair. Or if you have a mare and a gelding and turn them out together for a long period, perhaps several years, they too may in time think as one.

A truly empathic pair is a pair of horses who literally think as one, the perfect union. The nearest analogy I can think of is that of a pair of tuning forks. If you strike one tuning fork, it will hum, and if you put an exactly similar tuning fork beside it that will also begin to hum, in unison. If the second fork is not exactly similar – that is, it makes note D while the original is an E – the response will be less marked. And the further the second fork is from the note of the original tuning fork, the less the responding tuning fork will hum. So it is with e.s.p. and empathy : if you apply a stimulus to one horse of an empathic pair, the other, even though he is not in physical contact, will respond too. The less the sympathy between the two horses – the further from an empathic pair – the less the response will be, until two horses which are not in mental communication at all will make no response whatever !

I had my first experience of this phenomenon when I was quite young. Along with Beauty we had other ponies, and one pony we had had for a very long time was called Bill the Baby. When Bill did not want to be caught, we could not catch Beauty, and countless times I have driven Beauty and Bill into the corner of the field to try to catch them. I would approach them, and they would be standing quietly and quite happily looking at me, until I got to within five or ten yards of them, and then, without any signal I could see at all, one would shoot to the left of me and the other to the right of me, and on no occasion did they both try to go the same way. They would always start at exactly the same instant, so that there was no possible way of stopping them, and it was a good twenty years before I realized how they did it. I used to spend hours and hours trying to work out the signals that they were giving, so that I could stop them beforehand, but I never could. I can read those signals to a certain extent now, but now I know enough never to corner a horse if I want to catch it. I always make him come to me.

There is still a great deal of work to be carried out into exactly how one horse communicates with another horse using e.s.p., and into how a human being can communicate mentally with a horse or with another human being. Equally, we know little about why one person has this faculty and not another. The Russians and Americans have done a lot of work on e.s.p. and telepathy between human beings, mainly on telepathy, which is by far the less common phenomenon. But there has been very little work done on e.s.p. between animals, apart from our own. And we, I must emphasize, have only scratched the surface of the subject. We have researched only into communication between horse and horse, and horse and man. But we have found that if one is to do any animal-communication research, it is essential to concentrate in the beginning on one animal, and it must be an animal that has been selected as the one you are naturally mentally in tune with. Equally, if you are carrying out research into communication between two horses, it is essential to get two horses of similar breeding and type, and two horses that are naturally mentally in tune with each other.

We can sometimes find two horses with a natural empathy when we go to a sale; if we see two horses which come from different places yet are immediately friendly to each other, and start whickering and talking to each other, we know these two horses are mentally in tune. Normally, if you walk down the line of horses at a horse sale, you will see that most of the horses are standing in apparent mental and physical isolation from the horses on either side. But just occasionally you will see two horses, usually of similar type and breeding, who are acting in a friendly way and talking to each other. These are likely to be a naturally empathic pair.

In the wild, when a strange horse approaches, the natural reaction of the herd is to reject it; and to begin with, even a domesticated horse, if you introduce a strange horse to it, will react by snapping at him or telling him to bugger off. He will in fact be saying 'this is our home, you get the hell out of here, this is our territory.' This is the natural and automatic reaction of a horse, just as it is with human beings, who tend to reject advances from strangers. As evidence of this, you have only to look at a bunch of people travelling in a railway carriage, each sitting in defensive isolation. A naturally empathic pair, however, will drop their reserve at once.

It is only when you have obtained a horse that you think you are mentally in tune with, and obtained a companion horse which is also in tune with him, that you can start your research. You will start by concentrating on trying to communicate mentally with your subject, and at the same time observing his behaviour with his companion.

The first horse that I knew I had this empathy with was Weeping Roger. I have already briefly described the extraordinary circumstances in which I met him, one day in Exeter market. I was just having a look, and talking to a friend of mine, when suddenly behind me I could feel dejection invading my mind and body as if someone or something was screaming 'for God's sake get me out of here.' I turned around, and there was a horse just waiting to go into the ring, a dirty-brown lop-eared half-starved sixteen-two thoroughbred. I just had to buy him. My wife, who was standing some distance away, saw what was going to happen, and, realizing that a desperate illness required a desperate remedy, saw a very attractive girl, to whom she had just been introduced. By this time Roger was in the ring, and I was bidding for him. She grabbed this unfortunate female and dragged her over, hoping to distract me from the horse. The poor girl got one glance from me, 'hello', and I turned my back and went on bidding. Fortunately no one else wanted a lop-eared sixteen-two half-starved thoroughbred and I got him for £40.

I took him home, having learnt he had been on Exmoor all winter (this was the end of February). I put him inside and started stuffing food into him. I took him out hunting with the hounds three or four days later, and he loved it and I hunted him a dozen times more before the end of the season. Then just ten days before the local point-to-point at Cotley, the horse I had been going to ride in the hunt race died. So I entered Roger.

On the day of the point-to-point, I was so ashamed of his condition and appearance that I did not take him out of the lorry until the very last minute, and then took him straight down the paddock, once round, and down to the start. I always had a half-crown bet on the race with my friend Pat Frost, on who would finish first. But this time I had so little confidence in my mount that I made the condition that the loser would have a double scotch afterwards. I thought I was being very smart. There were about a dozen to fifteen horses in the race as far as I can remember, and they were off to a very ragged start, but away we went with me settling Roger down on the tail of the field.

On the Cotley course, you go first about half a mile uphill, then you turn downhill towards the finish, then away uphill again. By the time we got to the top of the hill the first time, I was two lengths behind the last horse, but Roger was going very well, taking his fences with great enthusiasm, and as we went down the hill, I was surprised to find that I was still in reasonable touch with the bulk of the field. Down past the finish, to the bottom of the hill, and away up the hill again – then the horse just in front dropped back past me, and I thought 'well that is good, I will not be last anyway.' Then we passed another horse and another and another. By the time we got to the top of the hill there were only two horses in front of me, and I thought I had better do something more vigorous, since Roger was hardly sweating. So I set him alight, and went in pursuit of the two riders half a fence in front of me, and slowly and remorselessly I found I was catching up with them. Three fences from home, the horse that was lying second fell, and by the time we reached the winning post I was within three lengths of the winner. I just could not believe it, that this skeleton of a horse had beaten some of the best horses in the West Country. Roger literally danced past the winning post, as if he had won the Grand National, his head and tail up and never more than one foot on the ground at a time. We went into the unsaddling enclosure and it took me five minutes to get the saddle off, he was dancing around so much with pride and excitement.

After this I really set about getting him fit to race, for I suspected I had a very good horse indeed. After breakfast each morning I used to take him out for exercise, and since it was very cold weather and I never had gloves with me, I used to put my hands into my pockets and they stayed there until I got home. I would direct him and control him entirely by e.s.p. I could make him trot, walk, turn left, turn right entirely by mental concentration.

Roger had another very useful function. He was a superb nursemaid. My daughter Paddy, who was then about eighteen months old, used to love horses, and the sure way of keeping her quiet and happy was to put her on the straw in Roger's box, and let her play under the manger and around his feet. She learned to walk by pulling herself up by his tail, tottering from one leg to another. When she fell down and bumped herself, Roger would blow at her, and she rolled over on her back quite happy again.

But we could never get any condition on him, and we were always ashamed to take him racing because he looked so terrible in the paddock, and the only consolation we had was that the worse he looked in the paddock, the better he was going to run. If he stumbled around and looked as though he would have a job to totter down to the start, we knew that he was really going to go that day, and we could get our money on. I won two or three races on him, and I always enjoyed riding him, because he was such a fantastic jumper, and he was so enthusiastic about racing.

Shortly after the Cotley point-to-point, a friend offered to buy him off me for £300. I did not want to sell, but I had him vetted anyway, to insure him. The vet, Bill Martin, checked his legs in the stable, then had him out to check his heart while he was standing still. He listened for two seconds and said, 'for God's sake put the bloody thing back into the stable before he drops dead.' Then I listened, and it was the most irregular heartbeat I had ever heard. It sounded like Victor Sylvester giving a dancing lesson, slow, slow, quick-quick, slow, but it was less regular than that, it would beat very very quickly and then very very slowly. How he ever walked, let alone raced, I could not understand. But since Bill said that he was as likely to drop dead walking around the field as racing, and the old man loved racing, we decided to go on racing him. When we left Devon to come up to Wales, he was sold for a nominal price to an acquaintance who wanted a horse for his son to start point-to-pointing on, and he ran his last race only eight years later at the Cotley point-to-point, when he was seventeen years old, and came second again.

I was always at one with him. On one occasion he woke me up at three in the morning. I simply knew there was something wrong, and when I went out to have a look at him I found that he was having a violent attack of colic. And once I found I could get through to him, I started trying to get through to other horses, by concentrating all my attention on the horse I was trying to get through to – leaving myself as I put it, on an open line to the horse. And after working at it for about fifteen years I find I can get through to nearly everything, except small ponies.

Mine is not a unique experience. After all, as we have seen, the bond between man and horse goes back to antiquity, and stories about this bond go back beyond the history of the written word. The story I like best, which seems to express the essence of all the legends about the faithful steed, is that told about a French soldier, during one of Napoleon's battles against the Austrians. He was wounded and lying in a field, when suddenly his horse, which he had not been riding that day because it was lame, appeared beside him, having broken away from the horse lines. The soldier pulled himself up on to its back, and the horse carried him back to his unit, where he was received by his comrades unconscious across the horse's bare back, without bridle, halter or saddle.

Man's ability to be at one with the horse is also well illustrated by the story of the American slave who used to catch wild mustangs by going naked into the district where the herd of horses roamed, and live and move as a member of the herd. He would start off by approaching within two or three hundred yards of the herd and just staying there. When the horses moved, he moved with them. When they went to water, he went to water. When they grazed he would lie down beside the grazing herd. He would fetch his own food from a tree a mile or so away from the herd, where it was left for him. Within a fortnight or so he would be moving in amongst the wild horses and be accepted as a member of the herd. Then, when he had established his position he would half-drive, half-lead the mustangs into an already prepared corral. Simply by acting as a horse acted, thinking as a horse thought, behaving as a horse behaved, and having no contact with man, he gained the horses' trust and could single-handedly catch a complete herd of wild horses.

8: *On Gentling Horses*

It seems incredible to me that, apart from my own work, no research has been done into communication between horses, of any type, and very little into the central problem of controlling horses: that is, into what is the best form of communication between man and horse. The state of our knowledge of how to communicate even with the horses we ride is very poor indeed: we know that if you hit an animal it will run away; if you pull its mouth it will tend to stop; if you pull its head left it will tend to go left, and if you pull its head right it will tend to go right. Modern-day horsemanship is a development of these four facts, together with the refinement that you can teach your horse to respond to a verbal command, if that command is repeated again and again. This is essentially the procedure known as 'training' a horse. The fact that the early form of training is known as 'breaking' just about sums up man's attitude towards the horse.

Breaking a horse is based upon three principles:
- (a) That if a horse responds wrongly to a stimulus, he should be punished;
- (b) That if he responds correctly to a stimulus he should be rewarded; and
- (c) That basically he must be made to do what you want him to do, by force if necessary.

A comparatively few horses have had a considerable amount of time spent on them, using this method of training; and the method, confined as it must be to the few and expensive has been written about at length. But even today the bulk of horses are trained by cruder and cheaper application of the same principles – a brave and hardy boy sits the horse until he is bucked off again, and the horse is forced

The author's 'gentling' method of training

Catching a horse by making him come to you: the author leads the horse with a bucket of food

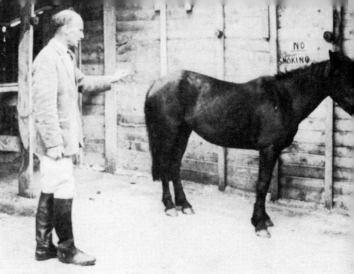

Calming a frightened or hostile horse, first by gentling with the voice: the author approaches, talking quietly to the horse in a sing-song voice

Using finger-tips he gets near enough to caress the horse with the tips of the fingers, simulatin the mother's muzzle reassurin a foal

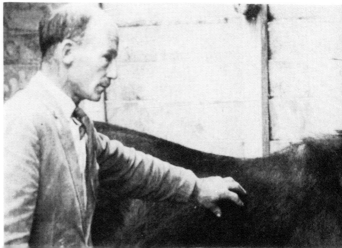

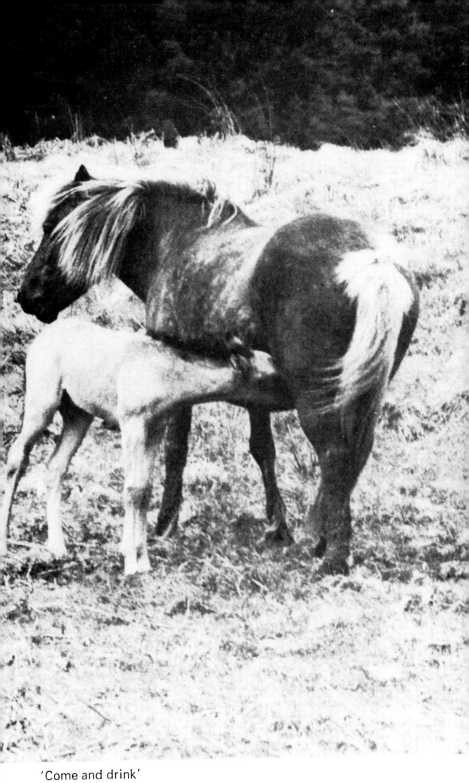

'Come and drink'

'Go away, I'm a good girl': the mare refuses the stallion

'I like you': he approaches another mare

'Let's make love'

'You'll be quite safe with me': he reassures her

And she complies: 'Come on then!'

Above and Right: 'Empathic pairs'

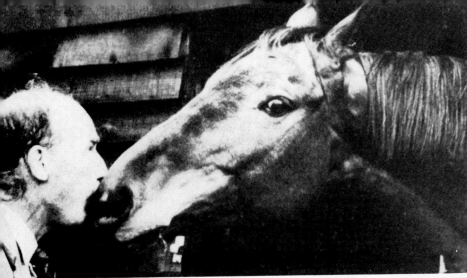

Above: 'Welcome': the author's greeting from his horses

Right: 'I love you'

'I'm boss': the grey tries to overtake the herd leader

'Go back': the herd leader gives the grey a nip to send him back into line

'Go away, I'll pulverize you'

'I'm hungry': foal approaches mother

'Mummy loves you, you'll be quite safe'

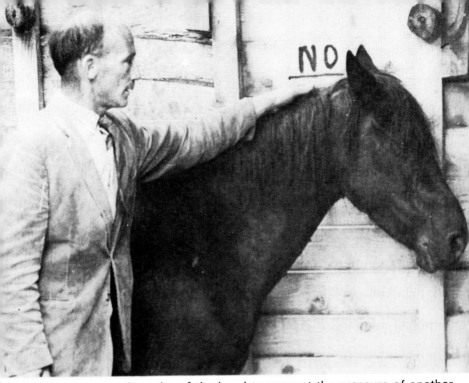

Above: Now he uses the palm of the hand to suggest the pressure of another horse's head

Below: Then he leans over the pony's neck, imitating the reassurance of the presence of another horse

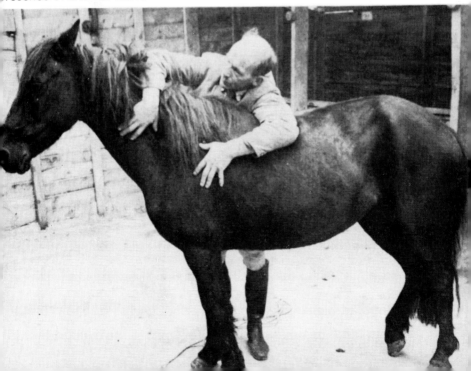

The author's wife, Leslie, takes a cross-country fence on 'Rostellan'

The author on 'Irefais Comet'

'Where's my bloody breakfast?'

to do what it is told to do until, by trial and error and various rewards and punishments, it has been trained to be ridden or to work in a cart. This system is to my mind entirely without logic, since it is generally assumed that the horse is less intelligent than man (though I admit that at times I doubt this). It seems to me to be obvious that it would be quicker and more efficient for a man to learn the form of communication the horse understands best, rather than to try to teach the less intelligent being the form of communication man knows best.

Our own experience has taught us that it is infinitely easier to train a horse, and you can get some very startling results, when you use equine communication methods. For the past thirty years, first with my father and later on with my wife and daughter, I have been handling and retraining horses that other people had given up as unbreakable and unmanageable. Many of these would otherwise have ended up in tins of cats' meat, or on the slabs of the continental butchers. These have been, generally, of two types. The first type are very intelligent horses who have been frightened and brutalized by ill-treatment. In the early days these were much the largest group that we got. Today, most of the horses we get are in the second group – strong horses spoiled by weak handling, often by women for whom the horses are too powerful and too strong. These horses have been retrained by using two qualities, patience and understanding.

All our reserves of patience were demanded to handle a horse we had not long ago, who could not be haltered or bridled because as soon as you tried to halter or bridle him, he would rear up on his hind legs. There were two problems we had to deal with. First, the rearing had to be cured. And second, the original cause of his trouble had to be identified and remedied. It seemed that at some time or other he had been hurt by someone putting his hands behind his ears, for this was the thing he refused to let you do. You could put a bit into his mouth sometimes, but you could

D

never get the bridle over his head. We could simply have used a leather bridle and put it on from his neck, but this would not have cured the basic trouble, so I simply took him into a loose-box and began running my hand up his shoulder and over his neck. As I got near his head he went up on his hind legs. As soon as he came down again, I put my hand on his shoulder and went up his neck again, then up he went on his hind legs again. After about forty-five minutes I could run my hand up his neck as far as his head, stopping short of his ears. So I began running my hand up the crest of his mane, until I got behind his ears – up on his hind legs he went. But I persisted, and after about twenty minutes I could run my hand up his neck, over his ears and down his nose. When I got to this stage, my hand went from his nose, rubbing his head, up to his eyes, and as soon as I got near his ears he was up on his hind legs again. But after another five or ten minutes I could actually run my hand up his nose, over his ears and down his neck.

Then came the next stage. I got a rope halter, put it on over his nose, then ran my hand up his nose and over his ears as if I were trying to put the halter on. He reared again so I took the halter off and tried to put it on again. As soon as I had the nose piece on I once more ran my hand up his head and over his ears. After a further five minutes of this I could slip the halter on and off. When he went up on his hind legs I took very little notice. I just went on talking to him all the time in a soft sing-song voice, and in a very short time, he was beginning to settle. He had ceased to be worried about my hand running over his ears; but at the same time he was damned if he was going to let me do it easily, because he had never let anyone do it. When I could get the halter on and off without any difficulty, which took about twenty minutes from doing it the first time, I went and got a bridle, put the bit in his mouth with some difficulty, took the bit out of his mouth and put it in again, in and out, in and out until I could slip the bit into his mouth whenever I wanted to. Then I ran the reins up his head and over his ears. Up he went on his hind legs, off with the reins once more, then back on with the reins. Then I put the bit back in his mouth, put the reins over his head and began to put the bridle over his ears. Up he went on his hind legs, so off with the reins and out with the bit, then on with the reins, in with the bit, and up with the bridle. I went on doing this for about ten minutes until I could put that bridle on and off whenever I liked. I had been at him for about four hours then, so I gave him a drink and his dinner and went to have my own. It was a very light dinner, it always is when I am handling difficult horses, then I went out again and started all over again. After about an hour going at him a second time, I could put the bridle on and off whenever I wanted to. So I left him for the day.

The next day I had him in again and went through the same procedure, which took me an hour and a half in the morning, half-an-hour in the afternoon and ten minutes in the evening. Within a week he took no notice at all of the bridle being put on and I could do it whenever I liked. It was patience that did the trick, and of course basic understanding of what the problem was. At the same time I had to be confident that I was going to succeed, and never get worried or excited. My attitude the whole time was calm, so that while dealing with his stubbornness I did not have to deal also with a frightened or worried horse.

It must always be remembered of course that if you have a very strong powerful horse, or a very intelligent horse, he will never be a ride for an inexperienced beginner, unless he is well and truly 'broken' – that is to say, unless his spirit is broken entirely. Since there is an endless supply of horses which are neither big and strong nor extremely intelligent, it is surely much better for the inexperienced or the weak rider to get a horse that suits his temperament, rather than to try to break a horse of a temperament unsuitable for his purpose. By the same reasoning, when we are expecting a horse to do cross-country work, we select a horse which naturally enjoys jumping and wants to go across country, since it is infinitely easier to get him jumping and going across country than the horse that wants neither to jump nor to go out for a walk. Similarly someone who does not want to go out for a walk should get a horse that is the same way inclined, not one that wants to go as soon as its feet touch the grass.

One example of how understanding comes into play when we are retraining a difficult horse is our experience with Jimmy, who came to us very recently. Jimmy had got on top of his owner, and there were a number of things that she could not do with him. To teach Jimmy who was boss, we used pure animal communication. Now if you see a bunch of horses going down the road, the boss horse will be in front. If one of the others in the herd tries to pass the boss, he will say 'go back' by swinging his head round and punching the offender with his teeth. It looks as though he is biting him, but in nine times out of ten he will merely be punching him with his teeth – he will only bite if the horse persists in trying to pass. So I took Jimmy out on a halter and every time Jimmy tried to pass me, I swung my fist round as if to punch him. I never actually connected, but I threatened to punch his teeth in if he tried to pass me.

After three or four days of this Jimmy very clearly understood that he could not pass me no matter how much he wanted to, so he would walk behind me quietly and obediently. A very difficult and strong horse, who previously dominated his owner, thus learnt that I was boss and not he. Jimmy had been taught to obey the orders of the boss of the herd, and because I had used a communication method that he understood he was neither frightened nor cowed by it.

It seems to me that the whole essence of getting the maximum of which he is capable out of the horse is communication. It is essential for the rider to be able to convey his wishes explicitly to the horse, and for the horse to respond to those wishes, so it is only logical that those wishes should be conveyed in a manner that the horse most easily understands, that is, in the form of communication that the horse uses himself. This is where e.s.p. is so important, for by this method the horse can quickly and readily understand your desires rather than your commands. For example, a horse should respond when the owner is excited, and he should relax when you are relaxed. When the horse is a sounding board for your own emotions, then that horse will respond in competition or in an emergency instantaneously, and in a far more enthusiastic and willing way than if he is merely responding to a command. Similarly, a guard sergeant-major can teach a squad of eleven men to play football on command; but that team of footballers would never in this world beat a team of people who play together for the love of doing so, and respect each others wishes.

This is where I think that the modern method of horse-training is wrong, since it is angled towards the dressage arena where anticipation of the rider's wishes is counted as a dis-obedience. I believe that if you are to get the maximum from a horse, that horse should be trying to anticipate your wishes, to do what you want it to do before you actually ask it. All you have to do is be empathic with your horse, and he will anticipate your wishes, since he will know what you want him to do before you ask him.

Yet the whole art of modern training is to teach the horse to answer commands. The basic commands that you will want to teach him will take up to six months, and the more advanced work two or three years. We on the other hand have found that with gentling we can get a horse to respond within hours. It is extremely easy to get your horse to do what you want him to do when you are trying to get him to *want* to do what you want him to. And the short-cut to this is via e.s.p.. As we have already seen, ever since primitive man first made the discovery that Eohippus had other uses than that of filling an empty belly, man has been using e.s.p. to ride and control his horses, to a greater or lesser extent depending upon the rider and his methods of train-ing; and yet nobody has written about e.s.p. with horses, and there has been no research into the subject whatever. We indeed had been carrying out research into e.s.p. for over ten years before I dared mention it to anybody. And then it happened quite by chance.

My wife wanted to visit her family in Ireland, and since as usual my car had broken down, I asked my friend and neighbour Charles Thurlow Craig to drive her to the station. After seeing her off, we stopped for a drink on the way home. One drink led to another and after the fourth or fifth drink, I happened to mention to Thurlow, who is a very receptive person, that I could communicate mentally with horses and control them by telepathy. I expected him to laugh at me and say I was too drunk to know what I was saying. Instead of which he said 'that's nothing, I can too,' and we discovered that while he could communicate mentally with Welsh cobs, and not with any other kind of horse, I could get through best to thoroughbreds and near-thoroughbreds. After an hour-and-a-half we went home.

The following morning I was troubled by two things: first, by a rather bad hangover, and second, by a somewhat hazy recollection that I had been fool enough to tell Thurlow that I could communicate mentally with horses. So I went up to see him and after we had had one or two hairs of the dog, he confirmed that he too could communicate mentally with horses and that he had been doing it for a very long time, but had never mentioned it to anybody until the previous evening. Since he was somewhat unconventional anyway, he did not want to be classed as a raving lunatic.

For the next six or eight months, Thurlow and I talked off and on about mental communication with horses, but I did not mention it to anybody else until I went to the hunt ball that year. And hunt balls being hunt balls, by midnight I was not as sober as I might have been. By this time I happened to be dancing with a very knowledgeable horsewoman I knew, and I mentioned to her this ability to communicate mentally with horses, and she thought about it and said 'Do you know I can do it with Poodle,' (that was the name of her horse). In the course of the next two or three dances, she came to the conclusion that she had had this ability with three of the horses she had ridden over the previous thirty or forty years.

The point of this story is that the first two horsey people I mentioned the matter to, realized after some thought that they could communicate with horses. Yet the idea that there could be mental communication between man and horse was on the face of it so completely outrageous that I had to be slightly oiled before I could even mention it, and that after ten years of research. After this I mentioned my discoveries to one or two close friends, then slowly to a much wider circle of acquaintances, and I found to my amazement that very nearly without exception they could all communicate mentally with their horses – not with all their horses, but with some of them. This has been going on for some two thousand years, but it has never been written about and there has been no research into the subject whatever.

E.s.p. is the ability to perceive by means other than sight, sound, touch, smell or taste. In actual fact this simply means that you can sense moods and emotions, rather than see or hear them – we know that e.s.p. mainly concerns conveying and receiving moods, emotions, feelings and limited ideas. A horse instinctively knows the moods and emotions of its companions. It does not matter whether they are human or animal, they can be animals of the same species or animals of another species. He can of course to a certain extent use his sight and hearing as well, when he senses whether they are angry or frightened, settled or excited. But we know that he can also feel their mood instinctively because we know that he will respond to his companions even if they are out of sight and out of sound.

That there is e.s.p. between animals of different species is difficult to prove, but our own observations tend to confirm it. We once, for instance, had a bull and a gander who were absolutely inseparable. Even if the gander was out of sight of the bull, when the bull moved from one field to the next the gander would leave what he was doing immediately, and go straight to where the bull was. He always knew where the bull had gone, even though he could not see him. The bull was running out with the cows and would come in and out with them night and morning, lying down in the yard while the cows were being milked. Sometimes the gander would sit on top of him or beside him, and sometimes he would go off and mind his own business. On one occasion he got shut into the feeding house, and when the cattle were turned out he was left behind. It so happened on this occasion the cattle were turned into a different field, about a quarter of a mile from where they had been grazing previously. When the gander was let out we thought that he would go straight to the normal field. Instead he ran out of the feeding house and took wing and flew straight to the new field where the cattle were grazing. This could have been coincidence. The explanation could have been that the gander flew at sufficient height to see where the cattle were. But it is within the boundary of probability that some sense told him that things were different, that there was some form of mental communication between the bull and the gander.

In another case there was a very close friendship between a cow and a pony. The odd thing about this was that the cow would know when the pony mare was horseing, and would mount the pony as one cow would mount another when she was bulling. Now there could have been no sexual smell from the pony that the cow would understand, and it is probable that there were no signs. Normally one pony mare will not mount another, so the behaviour pattern was strange to the pony and accordingly no sign would be likely to be given. Yet the cow would know instinctively when the pony was horseing. We believe that this very strong affinity between the cow and the pony caused a behaviour response that was natural to the cow and not to the pony.

Cork Beg had a very great attachment to a Friesian bull that we had, and they would stand together for hours on end. When the bull lay down Cork Beg would stand over him, and when the flies were bad they would stand head-to-tail flicking each other. The bull would use his rough tongue to scratch Cork Beg. At times they would play together: Cork Beg would stand on his back legs and strike out at the bull with his forelegs, then the bull would charge him, appearing to be hooking him with his horns. The first time we saw this, we fully expected Cork Beg to be damaged, but the bull each time he charged, would stop far enough from Cork Beg not to touch him. They would go on like this for ten minutes or a quarter of an hour at a time, Cork Beg pretending to strike the bull with his front legs and the bull pretending to hook Cork Beg's intestines out with his horns, until one or the other would get tired. Either the bull would roar, as if he were going to charge, and Cork Beg would gallop away with the bull in pursuit; or Cork Beg would dodge the bull as he charged and land two well-shod heels in his ribs, though without really hurting him. Then after five or ten minutes they would make it up and stand flicking flies off each other again. Now the curious thing about this was that the bull would know where Cork Beg was itching. If Cork Beg had an itch above his hip bone, the bull would lick there. If Cork Beg had an itch behind his ear, the bull would lick behind his ears. There was no way that we could see that Cork Beg could make the bull lick him. Further, this behaviour pattern was normal neither to Cork Beg nor to the bull, since it is unusual for cattle to lick one another, except for a cow to lick a calf, and certainly it is not usual for a bull to lick a cow except as a sexual stimulus. Equally it is unusual for one horse to lick another, though he may nip, or bite another horse to relieve an itch. Again we think that the two animals must have been communicating by e.s.p. But I would emphasize that this belief is based on observation and not on any real proof.

Two horses may or may not be emotionally or mentally in communication. We say that horses can think in different or similar thought patterns, and to some extent patterns tend to go with breeds. A thoroughbred will tend to have a thought pattern different from that of a Welsh Cob, and a Welsh Cob will have a different thought pattern from that of a pony, but there are Welsh Cobs who think as ponies, and thoroughbreds who think as Welsh Cobs. Of course these thought and emotional patterns are not static. If two horses have thought patterns that are mainly unalike but have certain similarities, close companionship will tend to increase the similarities, so that they will become closer and closer to each other mentally. We say that the thought patterns change and become similar. Again among a group of horses, those with similar thought patterns will tend to associate with each other, and their patterns will become increasingly alike. Hence in a bunch of horses, including, let us say, Welsh Cobs and crossbred thoroughbreds, the Welsh Cobs will tend to associate together and the thoroughbreds will tend to form a separate group. But they would also learn the thought patterns of each other. If a thoroughbred and a small pony are kept together, out of contact with other horses, they will have no emotional contact to begin with, but after a period of time, the two horses will develop an affinity and their thought patterns will become more similar. If, however, after a period of time other thoroughbreds and ponies are introduced to the original pair, the pony will tend to go back to its original thought pattern and the thoroughbred to his thoroughbred thought pattern. Thus horses of different breeds can learn by association to communicate with horses of different breeds, and with horses and animals of different thought patterns; but they will still be able to communicate most easily with animals who think in the same thought pattern as they do themselves.

This difference in thought patterns between horse and horse explains why a human being can get through to one horse and not another. It explains why one particular horse will do anything for you and you get an automatic response to any request, while another horse, even occasionally of the same breed, type and temperament will do the exact opposite no matter what you ask him to do.

Last spring I had two Cob-cross Welsh pony brothers to gentle. They were both by a Welsh Cob stallion called

Rhysted Prince, and a pony mare, and they were about twelve hands high, three and four years old, and strawberry roans. They looked almost identical, but one of those ponies, no matter what I asked him to do, would fight and fight me; while the other pony did whatever I asked him to do as if he were an old horse and had been ridden all his life. Yet when those two ponies went back to their owners, the one I could do anything with had the owner's son off as often as he liked to get on; but his brother with whom I had had such a lot of trouble, never put a foot wrong. It is the same with human beings; you meet some people with whom you are immediately in sympathy, and others who make the hairs on the back of your neck stand up as soon as you meet them. The French have a term for this : they say that two people are *sympatique* or not *sympatique*.

In our field of work on horses, the horses with which we have an affinity are those from whom we can get the greatest response. But we can on the other hand sometimes build and develop affinities by working at it when we are doing experiments between horse and man. I, for instance, have always been able to get through to thoroughbreds and near-thoroughbreds. No matter how difficult or awkward they are, they will always go sweetly for me, and I can very often get more out of them in a race than anybody else. But for a very long time, until seven or eight years ago in fact, I had no feeling at all for other breeds of horses, and my ability to ride or handle them would depend entirely upon my horsemanship and not on the horse. Over the years however I have developed an ability to switch wavelength to that of the horse I am riding. Even now I have no empathy at all with small ponies, and this I see as a weakness on my part, which I am hoping to overcome with perseverance and time. If you cannot get through to a particular breed of horse, you may find by working at it that you will be able to get through to one member of that breed, then to two, then three and so on, until with time you will be able to get through to most horses.

Over the last four years I have had the use, off and on, of a fourteen-two Welsh Cob, Trefais Comet, some of whose exploits I have already described. Now he is the most wayward bloody-minded little individual in the world at times. But I can get through to him, and he will always go for me, and if I am competing he gives every ounce of his ability and he is keener to win than I am. In fact he is probably the only Welsh Cob living who has consistently beaten thoroughbreds in cross-country competitions. He was second in a one-day event last autumn, beaten because he did a diabolical dressage with a score of a hundred and nine penalty points; but the cross-country course was extremely stiff and he was one of only three horses that went round clear, half-a-minute faster than the next horse and a minute-and-a-half faster than the rest of the field.

Being mentally in tune with a horse can have its drawbacks at times, however. I bought a grey thoroughbred gelding called Costa Clyde because I got through to him, and he was being outrageously cocky as he went round the ring : 'I am the best horse here, there is nothing else that can compare with me.' He turned out to be the most shameless liar in the world. Only after I bought him did I discover that he was always full of himself and his own importance, but he never made a racehorse and never won a race. But I was very fond of him and I used to love riding him, because of his supreme self-assurance and confidence. Even when he came back from a race, trailing in last, he would still be full of himself, and always have frightful stories to tell about why he had not won.

But it must also be remembered that by human standards the horse is of comparatively low intellect – its range of understanding is probably roughly comparable with that of a child of about eight. And it is the super-intelligent horses that are the most difficult to handle : they are the ones that often become unbreakable through mishandling, and get on top of their owners. On the race course they quickly learn that there is no profit in racing, especially in the tight finish, when they will get a hiding, and so they pack in racing and become dogs. But these are the horses we like, and these are the horses we get most response from with our gentling treatment.

9: *Proving E.S.P. among Horses*

Extra-sensory perception, as experienced among horses, and between horses and human beings, seems to have four different functions, which may be used separately or together. The first is to convey mood, which may be agitated and excited, or peaceful and relaxed. Now part of this message the receiver will perceive consciously, that is to say, he may see the horse's relaxed and peaceful swishing of his tail in the shade; but he will also feel his peace and serenity within himself. If the receiver is another horse he can be observed being made peaceful and serene by the first horse. But if something intrudes to disturb the peace – such as hounds going across the skyline or the sound of horses galloping – the horse becomes excited, and the second horse will become excited too, even if he cannot see the first horse and cannot see or hear what is exciting him. An observer will be able to see the second horse become agitated, looking around to see what is causing the excitement, *even if he cannot see what is happening to the first horse.*

The second function of e.s.p. is to convey emotions: anger, affection and so on. Anger is probably the strongest of the e.s.p. feelings: it is something you can feel mounting within yourself, knotting your stomach muscles, making you tenser and tenser until you feel you could explode.

I had evidence recently of just how powerful a message of anger can be. A friend had brought me an Arab-cross Welsh six-year-old for gentling, who had been used as a stallion for three years and then castrated in the spring. As soon as his wounds had healed, he was brought over to me, and I was especially interested because we had two of his sons at our place at that time. We named him Ieuan. I had an immediate affinity with him, which was rather unusual, since

I normally have great difficulty in getting through to anything with Arab blood. We worked him for about a fortnight, riding him every day and gentling him, and about Easter he was going so well and quietly we decided to put him into the trekking string. He went very well for three or four days, until a friend came to stay with us for Easter. He rode him on Easter Friday, and then on Easter Saturday she rode him again. My wife and daughter had taken them out, and they had been gone only about twenty minutes, when I could feel my stomach muscles knotting and getting tighter and tighter and I knew that I was getting a message from Ieuan. How I was so sure of that I do not quite know. So I jumped into my car and rushed after them, and when I caught up with them after a couple of miles I could see straight away that Ieuan was all over the place, just ready to explode. So I whipped Bill off his back and put my daughter on and they went off quite happily. That afternoon, however, Paddy had a young horse she wanted to ride, so I put Brian, another friend, on Ieuan and again away they went. And again after about half-an-hour I could feel my stomach muscles knotting, and off in the car I went and again Ieuan was ready to explode. As I caught up with them he started putting in a buck, but as soon as I got there he settled down and this time I put one of the girls on his back, and after that he settled quite happily.

On this second occasion I had felt the horse's anger mounting over a distance of three or four miles: a very remarkable event, since e.s.p. normally works only over comparatively short distances. This time there was in addition the unusual circumstances of a large number of witnesses to the actual working of e.s.p.

Physical sensations, such as hunger, thirst and pain are also conveyed by the horse through e.s.p., and the capacity to pick up such messages is something that all good vets seem to have. They can sense just where the horse is distressed and uncomfortable, and they use this ability in their diagnosis of illness or injury – a capacity which is clearly very important to a vet. For example, if a horse has a lame hind leg, it may be because he has injured his foot, his pastern, his fetlock or his hock; he may have pulled one of the leg muscles; he may have damaged his stifle or his hip joint; he may have pulled one of his thigh or back muscles or he may have damaged his vertebrae. And there may be no visible sign whatever as to where precisely the injury is. Of course the vet's previous experience will help him to guess where the injury is likely to be; but I have watched Bill Martin our horse vet in the West Country literally sensing out an injury. He would stand for five or ten minutes looking at a horse, maybe talking, maybe saying absolutely nothing, just looking and feeling. Then he would go, very nearly invariably, straight to the seat of the injury. I can remember him once saying to me, 'use your eyes and ears Henry, but also use your feelings.' He told me that he had a sixth sense that told him what was the matter, and I always regret that at the time I knew him well we were only in the very early stages of our communication work and I never talked to him about it.

E.s.p. can finally be used to convey very limited ideas, such as 'here is food,' 'let's go away,' and use is quite often made of it among horses. This function is probably really an extension of the capacity to convey mood and feeling, since, for example, the idea 'here is food,' does not come over in e.s.p. as a *message*, though it would come over as a message if telepathy were being used. What in actual fact the receiving horse feels is a sense that the hunger of his companion is diminished and from this he knows that the other horse is eating. Similarly behind the idea 'let's go away' is the simple fact that in flight the feeling of fear is being diminished. For practical purposes, however, I have found it useful to say that a function of e.s.p. is to convey limited ideas. The distinction is particularly useful when some form of reaction to emotion or sensation is involved; for two or three of these e.s.p. functions will often be used together. The phrases 'I am hungry,' 'here is good grass,' used together, come through as hunger and hunger diminished. The phrases

'I am frightened,' 'let us run,' come through as fear, and then the automatic reaction of flight, which is fear diminished.

This message-carrying aspect of e.s.p. has been vital for the survival of the species, since in the wild a herd of horses may often be scattered, with some members out of sight and sound of each other. But if one part of the herd should be frightened by the appearance of man, wolf or some other predator, the rest of the herd, maybe amongst the trees, can be alerted by e.s.p. even though they can neither see nor hear their fellows. Horses thus alerted will become first disturbed, then prick up their ears and snort, and start to move away from the area.

The horse will also feel the aggressive intention of another species, and this too has been vital for the survival of the horse. When for instance a wolf, man or other carnivore tries to stalk a horse to make an attack, even though he cannot see, hear or smell the enemy, the horse will become restless and disturbed. And funnily enough this is one of the abilities that has survived in man. If you try to shadow a man, you will often find that after you have been following him for a very short time he will start looking around, even though he doesn't know you are there, because he can feel you with a sixth sense. This is easy to prove for yourself. All you have to do is to pick on some unsuspecting individual in the street and follow him for ten minutes or a quarter of an hour. This sensitivity is one of the few elements that man still retains of his primitive self.

Over the last five years we have carried out a number of experiments into e.s.p. among horses. To do this we have used horses which were empathic, that is to say, pairs of horses which were at one with each other, who were close companions and who thought on the same wavelength and acted as one horse. They would graze together, walk together, and stand together and if you were trying to catch them, either both would come or neither would come. We used only horses which we knew came from the same source and had been together for two or three years at least, and, though this was not always possible, we tried for preference to select brothers or sisters, since we found that two brothers or two sisters brought up together tend to think on exactly the same wavelength. Before starting work with them we would observe them over a period of a month to six weeks to make sure that they always grazed together, and never palled up with another horse, even for a short period. This being established, and my own experience confirming that they were on the same wavelength, we were ready to select them for experiment. I sometimes found it rather difficult to be absolutely certain, from the e.s.p. messages that I was getting, that the horses were thinking on the same wavelength, since I tend to switch my wavelength of e.s.p. to the horse I am handling; but from among the forty or fifty horses we have through our hands each year, we tried to select two pairs of horses each year. After five years, we had selected eleven pairs: that is, we found the proportion of suitable horses to be about ten per cent. Of these, two pairs were eliminated because we discovered that the attraction between them was physical rather than mental – each of these pairs was a mare and a gelding, and they were sexually attracted to each other. (We deduced this from the fact that when the mare was horseing they were much closer to each other, and also much closer together in the ten days to a fortnight between her horseing periods.) The third pair we had to eliminate was an eight-year-old mare and a rather immature three-year-old gelding who came from the same farm, and had been to-gether since the gelding was a six-month-old foal. They appeared to be an ideal pair, until we actually started the experiments. I ran the five experiments on the gelding to begin with, and had a positive result in every case; but when I started handling the mare and not the gelding, we had a fifty-fifty result. Actually the pair of them came out higher than the average – 75 per cent positive, or 7–8 per cent above average – but after considerable thought I came to the conclusion that the mare was in mental contact with myself and not with the gelding – her affinity with the gelding was maternal rather than mental.

We were extremely fortunate from the outset in that the layout of the farm lent itself to the experiments. We had a loose-box next to the house, and fifty yards away, the other side of a range of buildings, we had a railway hut by the front gate: that is, we had two boxes out of sight and out of hearing of each other. Since when we were working on one horse, the other could not see or hear what we were doing, any response recorded had to be the result of e.s.p. and not of sight or sound. It was also possible from two points in the intervening building to observe the second horse without being observed; and provided we worked from the loose-box in the yard, the horse in the railway hut did not even know that we were in the yard, let alone handling or feeding the other horse. In the second experiment we had to leave the yard for a period of time, so we used the railway hut by the front gate to saddle and bridle the horse and take him out of the yard, and the first horse could not even see us leaving, though it was possible for him to hear our footsteps as we went down the road.

There were five experiments involved, and over a period of three days we carried out each experiment three times, varying the horses we were working on and the horse we were expecting a response from. On the first day we would use horse A, on the second horse B, and on the third horse A in experiment one. For experiment two the first day we would use horse B, the second day A, the third day B. On experiment three we would use A, B, A. On Experiment four we would use B, A, B, and on experiment five A, B, A. In this way we made absolutely certain that there was a fair spread of the primary and secondary response of both horses.

In the first experiment one of each pair was fed in the plastic container. For us to record a positive reaction his empathic pair had to indicate that he wanted food at the same time; and to make quite sure that there was no question of habit coming into this experiment, the horses were not fed at the same time each day, nor were they fed at their regular feeding times, so that any response had to be from e.s.p. On twenty-one of the twenty-four tests we had a positive response, which was better than we dared hope for: that is to say, on twenty-one out of the twenty-four occasions, when we were feeding one horse, the second horse, even though he could not see or hear us in any way, knew that we were feeding the first horse and demanded food. (Of course, before we carried out this experiment, we had to find out how each horse said 'where is my bloody breakfast.' Some of them bang their feeding bins, others whicker, two of them would walk from the door to the feeding bin and back to the door. One particular horse would stand with his head out of the doorway and shake his head up and down, up and down, until he was fed, and if you were a long time feeding him he would pull horrible faces.) This was the easiest experiment to do and to set up, since in the first place it is quite simple to eliminate signs, sounds and habit, and in the second place there is no question of personal opinion coming into it whatever. Your responding horse either says 'where is my bloody breakfast,' or he does not. There are no two ways about it. So to my mind this experiment is absolutely conclusive proof of the existence of e.s.p.

In the second experiment one of each pair was taken out of the yard and into a field, then excited by cantering and jumping and generally getting him hotted up. Positive results were recorded if, when the excited horse returned to the yard, the second one of the pair – who had remained in his box – became excited. This again is an experiment where it is comparatively easy to tell whether you have a positive result or not: if a horse is standing still, half asleep, and he suddenly pricks his ears and starts walking or dancing round his box, you may be absolutely certain that something has disturbed and excited him. Two of the horses became agitated and started whickering: in two cases the horse in the box became excited when the exercised horse was well over a quarter of a

mile away. But with another two – that is to say in three
tests, since one of the horses was used twice – we got no
conclusive results since the horse in question was a restless
horse anyway and tended on occasion to become excited for
no obvious reason. Nevertheless in this experiment nineteen
out of the twenty-four results were positive, with three further
results in which the second horse did become excited, but we
could not be sure that he was excited purely because his empathic pair was excited.

Experiment three was a more-or-less complete failure, because the positive results left too much room for human
error. This experiment followed on from the second experiment. After the excited horse had been brought back to the
yard and we had observed the effect on his companion, we
took his saddle and bridle off and went to his *companion* and
started gentling him and relaxing him. A positive result was
recorded, if the exercised horse relaxed considerably sooner
than normal. The difficulty here was in deciding how long
it would normally have taken the horse to relax. We had also
to shorten the series of experiments because one of the horses
we were exciting over-reached and cut himself, so instead of
gentling his companion we had to spend the next twenty
minutes cleaning up the wound and stopping the bleeding.
So we only had twenty-three experiments instead of twenty-
four. Out of the twenty-three cases we had eight positive and
seven marginal results, that is to say, in eight cases we thought
it probable that the horse had relaxed more quickly than
usual, and in seven cases we thought it was possible that he
had done so. I have included this rather unconvincing experiment in the series because I feel that with a certain amount
of scientific equipment, and considerable time to set it up,
it could prove one of the most definite and important experiments of the series.

The fourth experiment was quite simple. I would talk and
make a fuss of one of the pair, usually the one that I liked
least, and a positive result was recorded if the other showed
signs of jealousy. Jealousy is shown in various ways: the

horse might become disturbed and start walking around the box : she might (as happened with one of them) start banging at the door; or, like another lean upon the door, shaking her head up and down; and a third, as soon as I talked to her companion, started banging her dish. We took all these to be positive results, though they were not quite the results I expected. The curious thing about this experiment was that nearly half the horses showed a positive result by saying 'where is my bloody breakfast,' which possibly indicates that the e.s.p. message sent out was one of pleasure, which nearly half the horses took to mean that the first horse was being fed. Again we could get no definite result from the three horses which were naturally restless and excitable, because it was impossible to say their response was from e.s.p. and not from natural restlessness. But one of these was a mare who showed impatience by shaking her head up and down in the doorway, which was not the normal way that she showed her restlessness (which was walking around her box and then looking out of the door), but was the way she normally said 'where is my bloody breakfast.' We included this as a probable, not as a positive result. So in this experiment we had seventeen positive results out of the twenty-four.

The fifth experiment was a most unpleasant one, and I do not think I want to repeat it, because it involved really frightening one of the horses, and this is not a thing I like to do. I also think that it is possible to prove e.s.p. without fear. But since fear is a primary emotion, we thought it important to prove that it can be transmitted from one animal to another. I frightened the horse by rushing towards him, clenching my fists and chasing him round and round the box until he was frantic. A positive result was recorded if his companion became disturbed too. This happened in sixteen out of the twenty-four cases, plus of course the three excitable horses who could give us no positive result.

Out of one hundred and nineteen experiments we carried out in all, we thus had positive results in eighty-one cases; a marginal result in twelve more; and a possible result in eleven cases, which gave us an overall success rate of 67.5 per cent. When you consider that the only alternative to e.s.p. in explanation of these results is pure chance, it seems more than scientifically probable that there is a sense of communication between horses other than sight and sound.

We also ran a control experiment for our own interest. For this we used a mare and a gelding who were very hostile to each other, and among fifteen experiments we had a positive result in only one case. For this series of experiments we made absolutely certain there was no means of communication between myself and either of the horses – I did not like them and they did not like each other, and we were a very hostile trio! Thus, since in the control we had a positive result in 16.66 per cent of cases and in the experiment we had a positive result of 67.5 per cent, we again conclude that it is probable that e.s.p. between horses does exist.

It should be noted that the five experiments were designed to show the transfer by e.s.p. of the messages: 'hunger diminished', 'excitement', 'excitement diminished', 'jealousy', and 'fear'. What we have satisfied ourselves in the series of experiments is that it can be proved scientifically that e.s.p. exists. In fact if in our results you eliminate the excitable horses, and the failed third experiment, we have an overall success of nearly 80 per cent and not 67.5 per cent.

What interested us most in this series of experiments was not the results, which were slightly better than we expected, but the fact that they indicated the ability of horses to switch to other wavelengths. Some of the horses we used were horses of different breeds, who normally think on different thought patterns and on different wavelengths; and three pairs among the eight, what is more, were mares and geldings, whose thought patterns, because they are of different sexes, would again tend to be different. To prove that wavelengths vary between breeds and types, and that individual horses could communicate on varying wavelengths and in different thought patterns, we ran another series of experiments with four horses: a Welsh Cob, a thoroughbred mare, a half-thoroughbred thirteen-two pony and a Welsh Section B-cross stallion. The Welsh Cob was in communication with the thoroughbred mare and they were very close companions. The thoroughbred mare was in communication with both the Welsh Cob and the half-bred pony; and the Section B was on the same wavelength as the pony, but not in communication with either the Welsh Cob or the thoroughbred mare. After a very long series of experiments, we discovered that if we fed the Welsh Cob the other three all asked for food. If we fed the Welsh Cob and the thoroughbred mare was not there, neither the half-thoroughbred pony nor the Section B stallion would ask for food. When we put the thoroughbred mare back and removed the half-thoroughbred pony, the Section B did not ask for food. If we fed the Section B and they were all there, the other three horses would all ask for food. If we removed the half-thoroughbred pony at feeding time, neither the thoroughbred mare nor the Welsh Cob would ask for food. Again in this series of experiments we always fed at odd times so that there was no question of habit entering into the experiment, and we proved absolutely conclusively that the Welsh Cob, when he had food, was sending out an e.s.p. message which was received by the thoroughbred mare; who passed it on to the half-thoroughbred pony; who passed it on to the Section B. If we remove the thoroughbred mare there was no one to receive the message from the Welsh Cob, and so the other two did not know there was food about. If we remove the pony when the mare was there, she would know because the Welsh Cob would have told her he had received food, but there was no one to receive her message and tell the Section B. Conversely if, when the pony was not there, we fed the Section B, neither the mare nor the Welsh Cob knew anything about it. Put the pony back, the pony would be told by the Section B; but without the thoroughbred the Welsh Cob was completely in ignorance.

These horses were Rostellan, Iantella, Marie and Starlight. And Starlight's relationship with Marie made an interesting

story. We had bought him in a horse sale as an eight-year-old
stallion. We had him home and gelded him, then turned him
out with the other horses three or four days later, and he
immediately chummed up with Marie and proceeded to pulverize any other gelding in sight. Rostellan was petrified by
him after he had been clobbered by him the first time they
met. But apart from noting this affection for Marie, we did not
think any more about it. However eleven months later Marie
produced a lovely chestnut foal, which to us was rather con-
founding since he must have fathered the foal when he had
already been gelded!

This experiment is a difficult one to set up, since you need
a number of horses which are not all in close communication
with each other. In our case Rostellan could get through to
Iantella and Iantella could get through to Marie and Marie
could get through to Iantella and Starlight; but it is very rare
in a group of four horses for one to have no communication
whatever with two of the others. It is much easier to find
straight-forward empathic pairs. All these experiments however
have been designed so that they can be reproduced anywhere
by other people who have horses, and with very careful
selection of the subjects anyone should be able to get a high
proportion of definite results. Given a sufficient number of
horses to select from, and adequate time to make your selection, these results can be reproduced time and time again, and
we hope and believe that these six experiments will in time
be standard experiments for people who are interested in
proving e.s.p. amongst horses. We know that we are pioneers
in the field of equine communication, and being pioneers
we have to be very careful that all the work we do can be
reproduced by other people in other places at a later date. We
also know that the work we do now will be pulled to pieces,
and fully expect that in ten, twenty or thirty years' time
people will be saying 'Oh, Blake was all right, he started
early, but he was wrong here or he was wrong there.' It is quite
possible that in parts of this very extensive subject, we *are*
wrong. But in the field of equine research in general and in

e.s.p. in particular, we know that our work has been on the right lines because we know that we can, and do, communicate all the time vocally, orally and mentally with our horses. We can understand what they are saying at all times and they can understand what we are saying. We are in fact in the position of an Englishman who can speak French and can understand French. But at times he will be wrong in the elements of French grammar, and so it is quite possible that at times we are going to be wrong in the elements of equine grammar.

10: *Telepathy in Horse Language*

Most people treat telepathy simply as one of the forms of
e.s.p. But in this we feel that they are wrong, because telepathy is different from e.s.p. in that it deals with the transfer
of mental pictures, and uses the intellectual process, while
e.s.p. deals with the transfer of moods, emotions, feelings and
only limited ideas. It is a purely emotional thing and its
response is automatic. For telepathy to function it is usual,
but not necessary, for the animals to be of the same species.
And for human beings it is usual for transmitter and receiver
to be in mental and emotional, preferably also physical,
contact with each other. But telepathy in everyday life, while
it is comparatively common, is extremely hard to prove. It is
a spontaneous reaction. For example two people may think
of the same thing at the same time; but there is no method of
proving whether this is telepathy or coincidence. You may find
that you start visualizing a place you know quite well, only to
find at a later date that a relative or friend was at that place
at the very same time; but unless you actually recorded the
time, and exactly what happened at that time – what you
visualized, what you were thinking about – it is almost impossible to prove it. And even if you can prove the synchron-
icity, it is extremely difficult to prove that it was not a coincidence. Indeed, if you were to keep such records, you
would probably find the sheer number of coincidences – anything up to two hundred or three hundred in the course of
your life – puts the problem beyond the realm of coincidence.
But hard proof of telepathic communication remains extremely
hard to come by.

It is quite a common thing for someone to say 'I must
prepare food for the dog,' and the dog to appear almost
simultaneously by their side. With people who are very

close to their animals, this will happen almost every day. An acquaintance of mine came to live with her mother, and after she had been there for three or four months she began to wonder why the tea was always ready when she got home. The kettle had either boiled or it was about to boil. There was no question of a regular time, because my acquaintance was a nurse and the time she returned home from the hospital depended entirely on which shift she was on. Mystified, she asked her mother how she did it. Her mother said, 'Oh it is quite simple. I know that ten minutes before you get home Jojo will get up and start getting excited. She will go from her basket to the window and she will stand at the window until you get home. When Jojo goes to the window I always get the tea.' She worked out eventually that Jojo knew when she was going down a particular tree-lined avenue, about ten minutes from home. Of course sight and sound could be eliminated completely in this case, since she was still well over a mile away from home, so the dog could have known only by telepathy. This sort of occurrence is much more common than we are aware.

The Russians, who have carried out a great deal of serious research an telepathy, have conducted a very large number of experiments, one of the standard ones involving a pair of people in two different rooms, each with two tables in it. On the first table is a number of different-shaped and coloured objects. The 'transmitter' picks up the objects and puts them on the second table one after another. Then his companion, the 'receiver', in the second room will try to pick up the objects in exactly the same order and place them on his second table. In this experiment, with trained pairs, the Russians achieve about sixty per cent success.

Telepathy has fallen into disrepute in the West largely because it was the purported basis of thought-reading acts in music halls, and though no doubt some of these were genuine, most of them were fakes. But there has been increasing scientific interest in the field. The best-known people to conduct a telepathy experiment in recent years were an

Australian couple, the Piddingtons. Piddington discovered he had this facility when he was a prisoner of war held by the Japanese, and to entertain his fellow prisoners in the evening he used to demonstrate his ability with Russell Braddon, the author. After the war he and his wife travelled the world demonstrating their ability to transmit mentally over varying distances the shapes and colours of objects. On one occasion they apparently transmitted mental pictures of various shapes from a B.B.C. studio to an aeroplane.

Modern man appears almost completely to have lost the ability to transmit mental pictures, probably because this was the first skill he ceased to use when he gained the ability to speak. If you could describe with your voice what you were seeing, you did not need to transfer a mental picture. But some primitive tribes still retain the skill and we have seen that Laurens van der Post in his travels among the South African bushmen observed a witch doctor gaze at the cave drawing of an antelope, throw himself into a trance, and then so accurately describe the location where the antelope was grazing that the hunters could go out and kill it.

The ability does however seem sometimes to survive in civilized man at times of stress. I know of five cases where telepathy apparently occurred at the time of a motor accident, though in three of these it is not clear whether it was telepathy or e.s.p. that was involved. It is very hard to be absolutely certain, when asking someone about it afterwards, whether he actually visualized the motor accident at the time, or whether he was simply subject to unusual emotional stress. But there were two cases where the accident was described to me *before* the person knew that it had happened: in one case my wife knew that her parents had had a motor accident at least eight hours before she heard about it; in the other a friend of mine was told by an acquaintance that the acquaintance's parents had had a motor accident at the very time that the accident took place, some twenty miles away.

This then is what telepathy is all about: the transfer of

mental pictures. I have already told the story of how I discovered that I could direct Weeping Roger where I wanted to go just by thinking it. I would steer him to the left or right or straight ahead simply by visualizing the road. This was the first time I had consciously experienced telepathy with a horse. Since I used to exercise him for an hour-and-a-half to two hours a day, feed him, clean his box out, and groom him twice a day, I was in his company for three or four hours daily, to say nothing of passing his loose-box thirty or forty times as I went to and from the cow-yard. All this proximity strengthened the great affinity I already sensed with him. After this experience I discovered that with other horses too I could stop them from shying by telepathy: if I thought the horse was going to shy at something I would gaze intently at it and the horse would see it for what it was – a stone as a stone and not as a tiger about to spring, a piece of paper as a piece of paper and not as an eagle about to swoop. This is quite a simple trick, for a horse does not always see an object properly, especially if he sees it only out of the corner of his eye, and his natural instinct is to avoid anything that looks unusual or dangerous. But if the person on his back or leading him is extremely close to him mentally, the person can see the object *for* him, and the horse will also see it for what it is and take on the ride's confidence about it.

About the time I was working with Roger I was sent a grey gelding that was more or less unridable because he shied very badly and his owner could not do anything about it. After picking him up off the train at Axminster, where he had been sent from Ascot, I rode him home and to my surprise he did not shy at all. I kept him for about two months, during which time he always went absolutely perfectly quietly and never shied. I sent him back to his owner, who was delighted with him; but after about two months he was on the telephone to me again, to say that while the horse still did not shy and was absolutely perfect to ride, his blacksmith found it impossible to pick his feet up and shoe him. The point is that he was a very strong-willed horse, owned by a rather weak and nervous person, so the horse was working one trick after another to get on top of him. Once he found that if he shied he frightened the daylights out of his owner, he started shying as a habit. But since when I collected him from Axminster station I knew he was a shyer, and took very great care that he saw everything, he did not worry me at all, and by the time I got him home he had forgotten about shying at anything. When he went back to his owner he was completely cured; but he started the difficulty about having his feet picked up when he found that if he waved his leg in the air he frightened his owner. He was rather like a naughty schoolboy who jumps out behind a rather nervous person and says 'boo'. He just had a rather juvenile sense of humour.

Cork Beg provides further evidence of the horse's facility for thinking in pictures, for he could be kept in his stable simply by putting a thin piece of string across the door, and since he looked upon it as a barrier and could see the barrier, he would not come out, and very often we did not bother to put the piece of string up at all. On one famous occasion Cork Beg, who like all our horses was intensely curious, was in the railway hut with the door open. My wife was talking to someone on the road, and Cork Beg could not see them. He wanted to see them, so he stuck his head out. But he still could not see them. He leant out further. Still he could not see them, so he leant out further still. Now if he had not thought there was a barrier there, he could have walked right out, because the door was wide open. But he thought there was a barrier, so he leant further and further out until he overbalanced and fell on his nose and I had to put him back in! He could not come past the barrier in his imagination until my wife went and put a halter on, thus removing his mental barrier, and led him out through the stable door.

Horses in the wild use the telepathic facility to direct their companions to food and water, or to direct one horse to another from quite considerable distances. It may also be used to split a herd of horses in times of danger; you will find this

easily demonstrated if you corner two ponies that are difficult to catch, in the corner of the field. You will find that
one will invariably go to the left and the other to the right
of you, and they will try to go the same way only if you leave
them no room to go either side of you.

On a number of occasions we have had this ability to
transfer pictures rather dramatically demonstrated to us.
Cork Beg, who was in the field nearest the house, could see
us when we went to the feeding house and he would whicker
and say 'where is my bloody breakfast.' We would then feed
him. If about five or ten minutes later we went down to
where we could see the other horses, a quarter of a mile or so
away, we would be almost certain to find them all standing
by the gate shouting for their breakfast, even though they
could not have seen us or Cork Beg. We cannot be absolutely
certain that this was a demonstration of telepathy, though we
think it probably was, because it could have been a case of
e.s.p., so we did not use it as a demonstration experiment.
But one of the earliest experiments we carried out with
e.s.p. was with two small ponies who were particularly difficult
to catch. We used to corner them in a field and record which
went right and which went left, because we thought it quite
possible that one always went right and the other always
went left from habit, but there was absolutely no set pattern
as to which pony went in which direction. The one thing we
did find of interest in this experiment was that if we managed
to stop the ponies, when they tried again to shoot past us they
would change sides : the horse that went left would try to go
right and the horse that went right would try to go left. We did
not at the time attach any particular significance to this,
but it is quite possible that there is a telepathic element here
and a subject for future research.

Up to 1964 in any case we thought of telepathy as more or
less the same thing as e.s.p. Then the difference was demonstrated to us by Charles Thurlow Craig, who told us how he
woke up one night feeling uneasy and apprehensive, got
dressed and went downstairs, picked up his wire cutters and a

torch, put on his wellingtons and went out into a very black, dark and stormy night directly to the very spot, about half a mile from the house, where his favourite mare was caught up in barbed wire in a bog. He told me next day that as he went downstairs he 'knew exactly where the mare was and exactly what had happened' because he 'could see it in his mind's eye.' I made a note of the precise words he used.

I had a similar sort of experience myself the year before last. I had a thoroughbred two-year-old gelding called Royal Boy. Unfortunately he was extremely musical, and would stand all day by the window listening to the wireless and if the wireless was not loud enough, he would walk up to a pig netting fence and hit it with one of his front feet and listen to the tinkling it made. He would do this for anything up to an hour at a time, completely fascinated. We used to say he was playing the piano, and of course every now and then he would put his foot through the pig netting by mistake and not be able to get it back out again. After his first try he would stand still and wait for me, and each time I could see his foot stuck in the pig netting in my mind's eye and would get the wire cutters to get him out of his predicament. He always waited for me, and I am quite sure he could see me coming in his mind's eye. (Normally of course if a thorough-bred gets caught in this way he will thrash about trying to get himself free and probably cut himself badly.)

Once we started work on telepathy, we found we had to prove not only that it exists, but that it is different from other forms of extra-sensory perception. Thus we could, for instance, show one animal an object, usually a feed of corn, and record the response from a second horse outside of sight and hearing. If there was a positive response, we concluded that some form of e.s.p. was operating. But we could not conclude that it was telepathy. The mental picture of food in a bucket *may* be being transmitted from one animal to another, and if such a mental picture were being transmitted, there would be a response from the second animal, which would ask for food. But there is no proof that the communication is telepathic. As you may remember, we used this experiment to prove the existence of e.s.p., where no more than the communication of the feeling of hunger was involved. So we devised what we called the kit-e-kat experiment, inspired by one of the cat food advertisements on television. This was the first telepathy experiment we ever carried out and we used old Cork Beg as the subject.

Basically it was quite simple: he was offered two containers, each containing equal quantities of food, and I was to direct him to whichever bucket I wanted, merely by using telepathy. But the experiment itself took considerable preparation, because there were so many factors to be eliminated. Sight and smell were easily eliminated by using two exactly similar containers, with the same food in each of them. What was more difficult to deal with was the fact that most horses when free are left- or right-handed, usually left-handed: that is over a straight line they will veer to the left when walking freely. Cork Beg's deviation over ten yards was approximately eighteen inches to the left. So we took a line at right angles to the middle of his doorway, ten yards long, and the end of this line we took as the centre point. We placed one bucket six yards to the left of the centre point, and the other four yards to the right of it, so that when Cork Beg came out of his stable there was no bias to go over to either bucket, and without interference he did go to them on a roughly fifty-fifty basis. Now we were ready to train him to answer my telepathic commands, and this proved comparatively easy to do, if somewhat time-consuming. Each morning when I fed him, I would fill one or the other of the buckets, then I would wait until I was absolutely sure I was in telepathic communication with him, and mentally visualize the bucket that contained the food. Having done this I would let him out. Within a few days he was going straight to the bucket I directed him to, and I persevered with this for a fortnight. Cork Beg, being a very intelligent animal, quickly learnt that the bucket I was telling him to go to was the one that contained his breakfast.

Of course this experiment also involved a certain amount of training for me, since I had to train myself to use my will to focus my whole mind on the mental picture of the bucket, allowing nothing to distract me. And I also had to make quite sure that when he came out in the morning I was entirely in tune with him. But having made these preparations the experiment itself was extremely simple. For the first five mornings I directed him alternately to the left and the right. On the sixth morning, to make absolutely certain that he was not taking them turn and turn about by habit, I directed him again to the container on the left. On the seventh morning I directed him to the container on the left, and on the eighth morning I directed him to the container on the left. That is for four mornings I directed him to the container to which he had a natural bias. The ninth morning brought the most difficult experiment of all. For four mornings running he had taken his breakfast from the container on the left, and on the ninth I wanted to change him to the container on the right. Much to my relief he went straight to it. Having come out of that successfully, he had to take it again from the right-hand container on the tenth morning, from the left on the eleventh and on the twelfth morning from the right. Each morning he went directly to the correct container.

The whole of this preparation and training took approximately one month, and the experiment itself lasted twelve days. To operate this experiment correctly complete concentration is needed, the picture of the feed lying at the bottom of the particular container must be very vivid in your mind's eye, and above all you must feel the mental communication between you and the horse. The least little thing can distract you. A bird flying across your vision for just one second can break your concentration for another five minutes. But provided you get the conditions entirely correct, and provided you are in complete telepathic communication with your subject, the experiment itself is extremely easy to do. We had a hundred per cent success, when normally we would accept sixty or seventy per cent success as a positive result.

All the experiments we have carried out are in themselves extremely simple things to do. They have been designed to be simple, and inexpensive. Any research we have carried out has had to be paid for from our own pockets, so we have chosen experiments for which we can use the animals we already have about the place, and the buildings and existing layout of the farm. We have not been able to afford to put up special buildings, nor to buy the expensive electronic equipment which might have made our work easier. But this very simplicity has meant that we have had to be extremely thorough in our preparations, and extremely careful in our selection of the horses.

The research into communication by signs and sounds has been done through the very elementary means of making use of our powers of observation. We would see a certain signal and try to interpret the message; then when we saw the same message used again, it has either verified our interpretation or led to a new interpretation of the message. And so over a period of time, our observations have made us completely conversant with the signs and sounds used by that horse. And in our own communication with the horse we have tried to simulate the signs and sounds that the horse has used.

In our work on e.s.p. the experiments themselves are simple, the important and difficult thing has been selecting the empathic pair. With telepathy, however, the difficulty lies in devising the experiments. For though spontaneous telepathy is comparatively common, the difficulty is in getting any proof of it. Since telepathic communication is spontaneous, it is not repeatable under controlled conditions, and accurate records are extremely difficult to assemble.

We have been able to overcome the problem in the following manner. We verify telepathic communication by recording the time of the occurrence to within a quarter of an hour: a mental picture received must be recorded at the time it is received, and the horse you receive it from must be identified by the person who is receiving it. I usually keep most of my records on the back of cigarette packets, since I have always got a cigarette packet in my pocket, and I have not very often got a notebook. To give one example of a recorded incident, at one forty-five on the nineteenth of January 1972, I was sitting in my car in the car park in Llandeilo. It was a very cold but clear day, if somewhat overcast, and suddenly in my mind's eye I could see my wife and the two labradors walking down the road to a field in a snowstorm. I could also see my grey hunter Iantella, and my wife's second hunter Rostellan standing in the field. I could not see old Cork Beg, therefore I knew that I was receiving telepathic communication from Cork Beg, and I made a record of it. On returning home an hour and a half later, I established from my wife that the weather had looked bad, and she had decided to get the horses in. On her way down to the field it had started to snow, and she confirmed that she had had both dogs with her. She had also noted the time as one-forty when she left the house, since she had to get to the library by two o'clock. Since I had recorded this incident on paper, I knew I was receiving telepathic communication from Cork Beg. But the problem, as you can see, is first to record the incident yourself as soon as you receive the communication, and second – which is far more difficult – to make sure that you have someone else involved who has noted the time that the incident happened. Probably no more than ten per cent of telepathic communications will really be verifiable in this way, even when you are master of your subject.

We have recorded three occurrences over distances varying from fifteen to eighteen miles – the longest distance over which we have had any telepathic communication is approximately two hundred and forty miles, but we could not list this one as verified since the person with the horse at the other end knew only that the incident happened 'late in the afternoon' so we had no accurate time check. (It involved the serving of a mare. The owner of the mare 'saw' the stallion some time between four forty-five and five o'clock. When she rang up that evening to find out if the mare had been served, she was told only that it had happened 'after tea'.) We also know of three incidents, for instance, of people knowing that their horses were dying. In the first, a friend of mine owned an old horse, and while he was away on holiday his wife decided to have the old horse put down. He was having an afternoon snooze when he was woken by his whole head exploding in a flash of light. When he returned home the next day he learned that the horse had died at about that time. He told me afterwards that it had been a very weird and odd experience. The second example was last October, when Cork Beg was very ill. We knew that he was dying, and at half past two in the morning my wife woke me and said 'The old man is going'. She had been woken from her sleep by seeing him in a very green field, completely at peace and grazing. We put on our dressing gowns and went down, and the old horse was just breathing his last when we got there. On the third occasion a woman I know fainted at the precise time that her horse was being put down five miles away.

We are still not certain of the extent of telepathy between horses, since it is extremely difficult to differentiate, in communication between horses, between telepathy and e.s.p. We are not ourselves complete masters of the subject. But even so, we can say with almost complete certainty that we can interpret what our horses are saying to us and to each other, and we can make our horses understand what we are saying to them. Since I am a practical horseman, any knowledge I get is put to use in my handling and training of horses, so I use e.s.p. and telepathy when I am point-to-pointing, or hunter trialing, or taking part in a one-day event. And becaue I use these things and I understand them, I can get my horses to do more in competitions than anyone would think possible. For example, last summer I took, for a bet, an untouched and unhaltered sixteen-hand five-year-old, and in thirty-two days, between August sixteenth and September seventeenth, I had him competing in a show class. I hunted him, I competed on him in hunter trials and on the thirtieth day I won a riding club novice one-day event. In this event he was within eight points of the highest points in the dressage, and he had a clear round in the cross-country and a clear round in the show-jumping. He was of course an extremely good horse, very receptive and an easy horse to handle, and I got through to him straight away – it was because I was aware of this that I took the bet in the first place!

11: *Putting our Knowledge to Work*

Probably the best illustration of how we make use of our ability to understand and communicate with our horses is the gentling system of training horses, which we have devised for handling and training unbroken and untouched horses. We call gentling the 'easy way' to train a horse, since it is easy for the human being to train a horse if that horse understands what you want from the outset. It is also easy for the horse, since you are using a method of communication which he understands. It is not easy in the sense that it takes less time, nor in the sense that it involves less work – it takes just as long to produce the finished product, and just as much work as the conventional methods. But it is easier than they are in that there is a lot less trouble and there is a lot less argument between horse and rider, and we like to think that it is much more enjoyable for the horse. Instead of saying 'you damn well have got to do what I tell you to do,' we say 'let's do this,' or 'let's do that.' To give you a human parallel, the difference is between a Guard Sergeant Major drilling a squad of recruits, and someone taking a bunch of children for a walk.

When we are gentling we do things only in the way a horse understands naturally. For example if you walk up behind a wild horse, he will go away from you forwards, but if you approach his head, he will go away from you backwards. Now this is quite simple and logical, and on this principle we have devised the natural response to very nearly any action, and since we use equine communication the whole time, the horse understands what we want him to do.

During the course of a year we will probably gentle between thirty and forty horses. Some of these are horses that have been handled from birth, others may be six-, seven- or eight-

136

year-old mares or stallions that have never been touched or haltered in their lives, and others again will be horses that other people have tried to break themselves and have failed with. We also get a number of really bad and unmanageable horses whom no one else can handle.

Perhaps the true merit of gentling and of the way we understand and teach horses is best revealed in our dealing with the horses we catch off the open mountain. Most of these have never been handled in their lives and are completely wild. And we get most of ours from our own mountain, which stretches for two or three thousand acres with another couple of thousand acres of forestry adjoining it, which means that the horses have a free range of about five thousand acres.

To most people it would seem almost impossible to catch an untouched wild horse off an open mountain where he has a run of five thousand acres. But in actual fact it is comparatively simple. Any one herd of horses will graze only over an area of two or three hundred acres. The horses will have their set paths and grazing procedures, places where they usually spend the night, places where they go to in bad weather and others where they graze and normally drink. If the herd is frightened, the horses will usually go in the same direction, ending up in the same place, and then they will go round in a circle and come back again. So the first thing we do, over a period of two or three weeks, is to observe the habits of the herd to which the horse we want belongs. We watch where he grazes, where he drinks, where he rests and where he spends the night, and particularly we note where he goes in bad weather, since in rough windy weather the horses will not be grazing on the top of the open mountain. Normally the herd will be grazing in an area of twenty or thirty acres, but in rough and wet weather they will all shelter together in one particular spot, usually on the edge of the mountain or in a corner by the forest. Once we have established the spot where the horses go, we wait for a very wild and wet night, and then early in the morning go to the spot, and slowly walk the horses into the nearest farmyard.

This is simpler to do than it sounds, since the horses will be rather cold and miserable, and they will naturally keep to-gether. We do not approach very near to them. As soon as they see us they start to walk away. We walk slowly after them, keeping away but edging them slowly in the direction we want them to go. When catching wild horses, we never run, we never get excited, we never raise our voices. We are relaxed, calm and slow in our movements, talking to the horses all the time, so that the horses are relaxed and calm. We never get too near them and we never allow them to trot. Slowly and carefully we edge them down a convenient road or lane and into the farmyard. The horses will walk into the yard quite quietly and happily, and then we slowly drive them into a building. This can sometimes be a time-consuming process, but you must be patient. First an old mare will look into the building – she will be the herd leader – and then she will go in, and then her foal will follow her, and the others will all go in very quickly. The whole time we will have been talking to them in a sing-song voice, gently and slowly. We can see the bunch of horses, who have be-come a little bit excited and apprehensive when they get into the building, visibly relax. When they are sufficiently relaxed, we start easing the horses we do not want – in a herd of maybe five, ten, fifteen or in very exceptional cases twenty-five or thirty horses – out of the shed by ones and twos, until we are left only with the ones we need for gentling. When the other horses have been turned back to the mountain, the horses we are left with will be very agitated, because they are alone, and probably for the first time in their lives. If there is only one horse finally left alone he will be belting round the boxes, screaming at the top of his voice 'where are you, where are you, where have you got to.' And when I re-enter the box he will be absolutely terror-stricken. He will dash round the box, pounding into the corners, anything to get away from me. All his previous experience with man has been frightening, and he has been accustomed all his life to putting as much distance between him and man as possible. I ease myself into one corner, lean against the wall and light a cigarette, talking to him quietly and gently all the time, compelling myself to relax, and by degrees I will establish a thread of sympathy with him as I begin thinking on the same wavelength as he does. I shall be using e.s.p. to relax and settle him. After a very short while he will stop in the opposite corner of the box for a while, and I let him stand there looking at me, breathing fire.

The Spaniards, when they are talking about bull-fighting, say that the bull always goes back to take up his position in one particular section of the arena, and they call that the bull's quarter. We find exactly the same thing is true of a horse. When a horse is in a confined space, he will make his territory in one particular part of that space, and we call it the horse's quarter of the box. It is usually the corner of the box opposite to the one I take, and after a very short time, he will establish that as his territory and he will tend to return there whenever he is frightened or in trouble. When he has settled in his corner of the box, he will start blowing through his nostrils at me. What he will be saying is 'who the hell are you,' and I will blow back at him, pitching the tone of the blow two or three notes below his, so in reply to his 'who the hell are you' I shall be saying 'who are you.' And by degrees he will soften the tone of his blow, and I will drop mine lower still, until he is saying 'who are you' and I will have changed from 'who are you' to 'hello'. When he too comes down to say 'hello' to me I start to advance slowly and gently towards him. His range of messages is always the basic message, 'hello', but the greeting can vary from the very aggressive 'who the hell are you' down to just the plain 'hello'.

When the horse has accepted me enough to greet me as he would any casual acquaintance, I can start moving to the next stage of the gentling. I walk slowly towards him, one step at a time, after each step waiting for him to relax again, until I get right up to him. In between blowing through my mouth I am smoking my cigarette and talking to him all the time : 'there's a clever boy, there's a clever boy, there's a clever little fellow.' I also aim to approach him at his neutral point, that is the point from which he has no impetus to go forward or back. If I go towards his head he will go back, if I come up behind he will go forward, but somewhere between these two points, usually approximately two-thirds the way along the body from his tail, will be his neutral point. I may frighten him or something else may frighten him as I approach him, so that he starts racing round the box again, and if this happens I return to my corner and we start again from the beginning. But it will not take as long for him to settle this time, and eventually I will get close enough just to touch his side with the tips of my fingers, and then slowly I work my fingers in a circular motion. This is a very basic thing with horses. When a foal is frightened he will run back to his mother, and she will caress him with her nose. To simulate this movement is very reassuring to the horse : in effect I am saying 'it is quite all right, nothing will hurt you.' Also when two horses approach each other they will stick their heads out and just touch each other with their noses. Sometimes they will touch nose to nose, and sometimes they will do it on the side. At the same time they will be blowing at each other. Or one will blow whilst the other touches with his nose. They will be saying 'who are you, where do you come from.' Then, provided there is no hostile movement, they will approach closer, and this is what I do. From caressing the horse with the tips of my fingers on his coat, I start caressing him with my hands, slowly working myself closer to him and talking to him in an even voice until I have got my body right up against him. Then I very slowly work my arm over his back until it is over the other side of him, putting considerable pressure and weight upon my arm. What I am saying to him now is 'you are quite safe, I am here.' When two horses are frightened, or when a lot of horses are frightened, they will bunch together, pushing against each other, and pushing their necks and heads across each other. They do this to reassure each other. They are saying 'do not worry, you are quite safe, I am here,' the more frightened and nervous horses getting reassurance from the steadier and quieter horses. Now since our necks are only six inches long, it is impossible for me to lean across and put my head and neck across the horse, as a horse would do. So instead I use my arm and hand to simulate the movement of the horse's head and neck. I use the tips of my fingers as a horse would use his nose, and I use the rest of my hand as he would use his head, and I use my arm as he would use his neck, so that at this stage the horse is understanding what I am saying completely.

Up to this point, I have used three of the four methods of communication. I have used my voice to reassure the horse, I have used signs and I have used e.s.p.. But the whole time the horse has understood what I was saying and exactly what I was doing, since I have used the language another horse would use, and my actions have been actions that he is accustomed to. At no time have I forced the horse to do anything, because he has always been free to move away from me. At no time, apart from the first time I went into the box, has he been frightened, and I have not done anything to antagonize him. At this stage I would normally leave the horse alone for two or three hours, give him something to eat and go and have my own lunch. I would then come back to him after lunch and go through the same process again. At the end of two or three days he would then accept me as another horse. The whole key to the method is getting the horse to want to do what I want him to. A young horse always tends to be nervous and curious and wanting reassurance. A foal will get this from his mother, who will nuzzle him, as I use my fingers. The mare wi'l be telling her foal it is quite all right. When I use my fingers in a similar way, I too am reassuring him. If flight is impossible for a horse, he will seek reassurance by physical contact with his fellow horses by bunching together, and I give him the reassurance of my body. When I get on to him at a later date, I will ease my body across him. Thus I will be increasing his confidence by giving him a feeling much the same as he will get from another horse leaning his head and neck across him. Each time and with each movement I am saying 'it is quite all right, do not worry.'

For the next week or ten days, I will follow a pretty set routine. First when feeding and watering the horse I will gentle him three times a day. Each time I feed him I spend ten minutes gentling him until he looks upon me as another horse, and treats me as he would treat another horse, and during this time I will be making a mental note of the sounds and signs he uses to convey each of the forty-seven messages – though in the normal everyday he will be using only about thirty of them. I will know I have finished this stage of gentling when I go out in the morning and he sticks his head out of the door and shouts 'where is my bloody breakfast.' If then, when I take the feed in, he pushes me out of the way to get at his feed saying 'get out of my way you stupid fool, I am starving,' I know he looks upon me as another horse, and understands and trusts me completely. I will also know by this time the temperament and character of the horse. I will know whether he is a nervous timid animal who needs to be coaxed and reassured all the time, or a placid easy-going horse that will do anything for a quiet life, or a very dominant and strong character. What I would do at the next stage of the gentling depends upon the disposition. If the horse is nervous and constantly needs reassuring we go on very gently and slowly, always moving quietly and always reassuring, telling the horse how clever and intelligent he or she is. The easy-going horse is also very simple to deal with. But about one in five or one in eight of the horses we get is a very strong, dominant character, and he needs a certain amount of discipline. Above all such a horse needs telling that I am the boss of the herd, I am the one that controls the herd, and not him. This message takes a little time to sink in, since that horse probably has been the boss of the herd where he comes from, and been accustomed to giving orders and not to taking them. But it is really quite simple, with a little time and patience, and by using the language the horse knows, to establish discipline in the method that the horse understands.

The way discipline is imposed within the herd is perfectly straightforward and is most easily seen in a bunch of horses loose going down a road together. The boss horse (often a mare) will establish itself in the front, and if anything tries to pass or comes too close, the boss will swing her head round, threatening to punch the offender with her teeth. At the same time she puts her ears back and says 'go back you horrible little squirt.' If the offender still tries to pass, the boss will then punch with her teeth. If the offender persists she will then bite him as he goes by. Thus if anyone offends the code of behaviour of the herd retribution is instant, and the incident is usually over in a few seconds. Even if the offender does eventually get by, the horses will settle down again quite happily walking one after another. So if I find myself with a very strong character, who when I am feeding her in the morning tries to push me out of the way and says 'get away you horrible little man,' I retaliate immediately by swinging my fist at her in exactly the same manner as she would swing her head at an inferior horse. As soon as I swing my fist, she will jump back to her corner in the box, raising her head and looking at me, saying 'what the hell did you do that for.' Then she will come forward quite happily when I put the feed in the manger. This will go on for two or three days. When I go out in the morning she will say 'where is my bloody breakfast,' I will take it in to her, she will try to push me away and I will swing my fist saying 'go back I am boss.' Within three or four days, without any real fight and certainly without frightening her, I have established that I am the boss of the herd, and she has to do what I tell her. It is most unlikely that at any time when I swung my fist at her I would actually make contact with any part of her body: I am only miming the threatening gesture. Then, once I have established my herd dominance, we are ready to go on to the next stage and for me to start mounting and riding her.

Horses come to us for gentling from all over the country, but mainly they come from within an area of fifteen or twenty miles. When they arrive it is not always convenient for us to gentle them straight away, so we turn the initial part of the work over to one of the other horses. We let the horses do an awful lot of the gentling for us. This is not quite as odd as it sounds, because all it involves is turning the new horse out into a nearby field with one of the steadiest and most established of the horses we have, who then plays schoolmaster. We will start feeding both of them every day. The first day when we take the feed down to them, the young horse will go hell for leather towards the far end of the field, while of course the old horse as soon as he sees the feed will come trotting over. Then we will put the feed down in two buckets about twenty yards apart, and talk to the old horse while he eats his feed, but not take any notice of the horse we are gentling. The horse we are gentling after a bit may come over to see what the old horse is eating, but he will not come within less than about twenty yards of us. When Jack or Tabby or Inatella or Rostellan, whoever it is, has finished his or her feed, we go away and leave them. Of course Jack will then go and see if there is anything in the other bucket, and proceed to eat that, but we go away and leave him to it. Then the young horse will come over, first sniff what Jack was eating before and then go over and see what he is eating now. After a day or two the young horse will start eating out of the bucket, and as soon as he is doing this, we start talking to him as well as Jack. He may or may not rush off to the far corner of the field, but if he does he will come back to his bucket. Within a week or ten days I will be able to go straight up to the bucket, talking to him in a gentle voice, blowing at him through my mouth, and possibly even get a hand on him. By this time I will be an established member of his particular herd, and he will accept me as a normal member of the establishment.

After he has been eating for about a week, we will start bringing the two horses into the yard for the bulk of their feed. This again is really very easy. My wife or someone else will put a halter on to the schoolmaster and lead him in, and I will get the pupil eating out of the bucket, and I will pick up the bucket and walk to the yard. Since there is still food in the bucket, the pupil will rush after me. Within a very short time, he will just put his head in the bucket, I will lift it up and he will follow me anywhere, and in this way I have taught him to be led even though I have never put a halter on him. After two or three days, instead of holding the bucket behind me when I am leading him in, I will hold the bucket in front of me, so that he is walking beside me. Then it is only a very small step to having him walking beside me with my arm over his neck. When I have got him used to this stage, I can lead him in by simply putting my arm over his neck, and he will walk up with his head under my arm, and then it is just one straight step to putting a piece of string round his neck and leading him in. At this stage, by putting the bucket on the ground, and letting him put his head into the bucket, through the nose of the halter, I can put the halter on him. Again, at no time has there ever been a battle. Always when I have been working with him, I have been talking to him in a gentle voice, and as soon as I can get my hand on to him, I have been gentling him with my hand simulating the movement of the mare's nuzzle with my fingers and hand and giving him reassurance by leaning against him and putting my arm the other side of his body, the way another horse would put his neck.

After about a week of this treatment he will know that the bulk of his feed is in the stable. When I open the gate he will try to push past me to get to his food more quickly. Again I will walk up the road in front of him, and as he tries to pass me I will swing my fist at him, using the sign he knows says 'go back you horrible little animal.' He will throw his head up and put his brakes on and say 'what the bloody hell is the matter with you,' and so we will proceed up the road. But in a day or two I will once more have established that I am the boss of the herd and not him, and when we go in he walks in behind me, and is not allowed to push past. Again at no time has he been frightened nor been made nervous or angry.

One of the most outstanding of our gentling successes was with a little mare called Spitfire. I first saw Spitfire as a twelve-three mare in Llanybyther market. She had a foal at foot and was supposed to be in foal again, and when she was driven into the ring with her foal, she went straight out over the crowd at the end. After a lot of trouble she was brought back in again, and a friend of mine bought her. I saw her from time to time over the next five or six months, until the following May my friend asked me to swop her for one of my horses. He confessed that he could do nothing with the bitch. It seemed he could not catch her, that she was not in foal, and he could not even get her to the stallion – he threatened to sell her at once for dog meat if I would not take her. I went up to have another look at her. She was a twelve-three thirteen-hand, very dark chestnut mare with a silver mane and tail and she was eight years old. She had had two or three foals, but she was now apparently barren. I could not see a strong healthy pony being shot like that, so we did the deal, and I went up at six o'clock that night to get her.

This was a mistake, because if you are going to do anything with a horse which you know is difficult, you should never do it in the evening. You should do it in the morning, so that you have all the day in front of you. She was in the field by the yard with a number of other ponies, and we made a lane into the yard with gates, and there were three or four people around with sticks, which I did not like, but I could not say anything because it was not my farm. They all got to the other side of the gates, ready for what they expected to be a performance. But we did not have much trouble. We drove her into the yard with half a dozen other horses and then, after some trouble, into a loose-box. She did try to jump a six-foot wall, but fortunately when she got her legs on top of it, there was someone the other side who caught her a clout and she had to go back. I discovered afterwards that she had previously jumped that six-foot wall five times. She had also jumped the iron gates which were over four-foot-six high, and later I was to see her jump a three-foot-six post and rails with a ten-foot drop the other side. My friend assured me that they had tried to get her into the loose-box many times before, but that this was the first time they had managed it. This was probably because we had taken the horses into the yard very slowly and very carefully, and instead of trying to chase them in, we had opened the yard gate, and let the other ponies of the herd walk in slowly. Since we were not trying to drive Spitfire in, she had followed the others. We were never within twenty yards of her. And once we got them all into the yard she could not jump out over the gates. Then we got them from the big yard into the small yard. To get these horses a matter of fifty yards took us nearly half an hour, but we never hurried them, just edging them the way we wanted them to go.

Having got the whole herd into the big stable, we then proceeded to let them out one by one. Three times Spitfire came to the door and tried to get through it, and three times the door was slammed in her face, but eventually we were left with Spitfire in a box about eighteen feet by fourteen. Now came the moment of truth, the time to halter her. So I went into the box with the halter and approached her, and of course she went round the box at a hell of a speed. When she steadied down I approached her again, and this went on for about half an hour, but gradually she slowed down until I could get my fingers on her, and as soon as I touched her, she swung round at me with her teeth and her front feet. So I punched her in the face and she retired to her corner of the box and I retired to mine, and we started again. Again after about twenty minutes I got my fingers on her, and she came

at me again. I punched her on the nose again, and the two
of us retired to our respective corners. This went on for well
over two hours, and I could see we were getting nowhere.
Each time I touched her, she attacked me, I punched her on
the nose and we retired to our corners. And since it was getting
dark I had to do something quickly. So the only thing I could
do was to get a fourteen foot gate and put it across the box.
Then I slowly edged her up to the wall. I got her about half
way up towards the wall, when Spitfire went back on her
hocks and come straight over the gate. So I started again.
After about twenty minutes I finally got her right up against
the wall, so that I could get my hand on her. I eased my
hand up her neck, she managed to swing her head round and
take a piece out of my arm, so again I went back. And as I
went back a little bit, she came out under the gate, lifting it
with her head, so I started again. Always talking to her
quietly, gently and peacefully, again I got her up against the
wall of the loose-box and got my hand on her and eventually
I managed to slip the halter over her head and tighten it
up.

Once I got it tightened and knotted under the chin,
however, came the problem of leading her out. But this was
not as difficult as it seemed. I put a second halter rope on the
one I had, and then let her out from behind the gate, removed the gate from the loose-box, and I let her go round
the shed past me. As she went past me I began shortening the
halter rope. As I got nearer to her she came at me with her
teeth and her feet, but I swung her past me and got into her
shoulder so that I was beside her. I managed to catch hold
of the halter right up under her chin. As soon as I had done
this, once I got my body beside her, she started to settle
down. And she quietened slowly until she was walking round
and round with me leaning on her. Then I led her out into
the yard and managed to get her up into the trailer without
very much trouble, tying her up short in the trailer so that I
could release her easily. Fortunately for me, while she would
come at me with her teeth and her front feet, she would not

kick. Then I took her home and tied her up in the stable for the night.

It is necessary here to explain exactly what the mare and I had been saying to each other. Once I got her into the loose-box I could concentrate on her and I followed the normal procedure of settling her with my voice and e.s.p.. When I got my fingers on her, she responded by attacking me: she had obviously been badly ill-treated in the past, and found that the only way of escape was to attack anybody who tried to touch her. So she attacked me, saying 'go back, go back, go back, or I will pulverise you,' in answer to which I punched her on the nose and said 'if you do not go back I will pulverise you,' until we both retreated to our own corners and we started again. Now given time, if I had started with her in the morning, as I should have done, we would have gone on like that for maybe four or five hours until I got my hand on her, and then I could have haltered her quite simply; but since we were running short of time and daylight, and the worst thing in the world would have been to have gone away and left her for the night and come back again next day, I had to resort to other methods to get her haltered, methods I do not normally use.

For the next week, three times a day, I fed her and watered her and led her around and gentled her and handled her, until she was relaxing and trusting me. What is more she stopped trying to make a meal of me instead of the corn I was bringing her. After that came the next stage: to try to halter her. But since I had her in the big building, where she had been tied up in one particular stall, I let her loose in the building and of course she went round me hell for leather until she finally went into the stall again. I left her standing there for two or three minutes. I walked up to her, getting her to relax, using my voice, and being relaxed myself so that I could use e.s.p. on her. Then I managed to get my fingers on her side, and slowly get my arm over her neck and put a halter on her. After this I started turning her out with the other horses by night, but of course getting her in was somewhat time-consuming, since even if you had a lot of people standing right round the outside of the yard she would jump the smallest to get back out again. But over the course of the next two months she gradually got better, until it was only a question of opening the gate when the horses came in, and she would walk up the road and into the stable. I never had any trouble riding her and from the first time I got on her, I could direct and control her entirely by using e.s.p., and she turned out to be a wonderful ride – and a fantastic jumper of course. But it took a very long time before she was coming in happily and it took me nearly nine months before I could shoe her without difficulty. It was because I always talked to her in a language she understood that she very slowly recovered from her hatred of mankind, and eventually became very fond of me.

The following winter she was turned out with the other horses, and by about Christmas she would come up to me in the field and take a feed out of the bucket, and I used to lead her into the stable with her nose in the bucket without any difficulty. By the end of June, she had settled down and was absolutely quiet, though she remained a very hot, keen little ride and was not suitable for a beginner. So I sold her to a young couple down in Glamorgan and they were very pleased with her, until the woman started a baby and the husband decided the mare was a bit too much for her. So they brought her up to Llanybyther once more to sell her. As soon as I got into the market I knew she was there. I could feel it. I went straight to the big stable, and there was my beloved Spitfire. I had regretted selling her, and could not let her go again, so I bought her back and she is now in foal to an Anglo-Arab stallion. I hope she will have a foal half as good as she is. She was a case for which gentling was the only system that could possibly have done anything. If we had not had her, she would have been shot.

Of course I much prefer handling a very difficult horse to one that is easy and straightforward. It gives me enormous pleasure when a horse which is completely impossible to

handle or ride starts enjoying his work and wanting to do
well.

It is only after I have got a horse going steadily and
quietly that it is time to start riding her. I do this quite
simply. When I go to the box on the morning I am going to
start riding a horse, I always go through the same routine.
First I start gentling for about five minutes. When she stands
still I get my fingers on to her just where the barrel begins
to narrow to the girth. She will twitch her skin, standing
with one ear forward and one back, while I go round and
round with my fingers. 'There's a clever girl.' Now the
second set of fingers, both hands flat into her body. Bigger
circles, lean on her, working forward and over the back,
both sides of the neck. She takes one step forward, so work
back a little until she settles, and stands well with both ears
forward. Now her muscles are relaxing, tension is going out
of her, mentally we are in tune. Work forward, up the
neck. She has an itch under her chin, so scratch it. Ready
now for the halter, work back, get the halter, work forward,
halter on from far side of the neck, over the ears. I tighten
the very loose chin rope and I give her to my wife to hold,
get the saddle with girth and stirrups flapping, put the saddle
over her and on to her. She tenses and walks forward. My
wife, who has been holding her and gentling her, keeps
gentling her, walks with her. I lift the saddle off, she stands
still. On with the saddle again, gently with one hand under
the tummy catching hold of the girth, buckle one strap
loosely, talking, talking all the time. Buckle the second strap
tighter. Tighten the first strap, now get the girth as tight as
possible. She will object and walk round the box, but my
wife is still with her, talking, gentling. She stands still. Tighten
some more, get the bridle, a soft egg-butt snaffle – ease it
on. Into her body, gentling her on her shoulder, on her
flank, lift my left leg. My wife eases me on to her, I lie
across her. She walks forward, I slide off, and walk with her,
until she stands. Ease on again, leg over, slowly upright, still
talking, still gentling, feet into the stirrups. She walks round

the box, she stands, my wife ties the halter rope round her neck, and opens the door and goes out. She follows, looks out of the gate to the road up to the mountain. Click my tongue, we will walk through the door, out of the gate, and up the road, my wife walking four or five yards in front. Forty or fifty yards up the road I say 'whoa-a-a', and pull the reins gently. My wife stops, and so does the mare. I click my tongue, my wife goes forward, and the mare follows. Forty yards, 'Whoa', and we all stop. Click my tongue and we start. After doing this three or four times, she will be stopping and starting on command, and so we turn round and go home, still talking, talking, still stopping and starting every thirty or forty yards. But my wife is now fifty yards behind us. Into the yard, and into the stable, slide off quickly and quietly.

When you are catching a young horse either in a field or a stable, or putting your hand on him, prior to gentling him, never approach his head, never from behind, always approach at a right angle, to the middle of the body. Get yourself mentally relaxed and in tune with your horse. If you and your horse are in tune, and thinking on the same wavelength, you can get away with an awful lot of mistakes. But if you are at odds with each other, you are in trouble from the start, and you will be fighting all the time. We always try to work our horses in a confined space, approximately ten foot by ten foot, because we find this gives maximum physical and mental contact, and at the same time gives the horse enough room to get away from us. Up to the time you leave the loose-box, you are using e.s.p., sounds and signs to relax and settle your horse, but to get movement and direction you must use telepathy as well. You visualize where you want to go, so that the horse wants to go there as well. The whole time you are trying to get the horse to want to do what you want him to do. In the early stages your assistant either walks in front of you or leads you. But you will find that the horse very quickly learns the words of command to which he naturally responds: a slowly drawn-out 'whoa' to stop, and a clicking of the tongue to start. He does not understand naturally words like 'walk on', 'trot on', though he will learn them later. The bit is hardly used at all, and you ride always with a slack rein. You settle well down in the saddle with your feet well home, to give you greater control if anything does go wrong. (The idea that there is only one correct way to ride a horse is wrong: you adapt your technique to the occasion. Terry Biddlecombe's steeple-chasing seat would win few show-jumping contests. Mr Laurence's dressage seat would not win Lester Piggot many races. And as was clear on television, Harvey Smith's show-jumping seat is a little insecure when riding round Aintree. So when riding a young horse, you require a seat adapted for that purpose: one that gives you maximum security, not one in which you have your bust and backside stuck out and your toes balanced precariously on the edge of the stirrup.)

The most important thing to remember is that the whole time you are talking to the horse, you are being entirely and completely natural. As far as the horse is concerned he is enjoying what he is doing and you should be enjoying it as well. You should be in tune with the horse mentally and understand exactly what he is saying to you. You understand what he is saying when he tenses his muscles, you watch the angle of his ears and any sounds or signs he makes. But most of all you can sense what he is thinking and he can sense your relaxation and your happiness.

The simplest way to back a horse is one we very often use, especially if we have a horse out in the field and bring it in every day. After we have been bringing it in for a fortnight or three weeks, I pull him in to the bank just outside the field and let him eat the grass on the bank. I lean across him and let him carry me to the yard. After a few days of doing this, I simply put a leg across him and ride him in and out in a halter. He takes it all as a matter of course. This is part of the natural habit of his life, and he is beginning to learn the signs and sounds that he will associate with his conversations with human beings. When he is quite accustomed to me riding him in and out of the field, it is only a very short step from taking him and his companion out for half an hour. I may do this riding him bareback in a halter, or I may put a bridle and saddle on him. When I start doing this I start teaching him to stop and start, but only in spells of three or four minutes at a time. I take the horse out with his companion every day for twenty minutes to half an hour, with two or three schooling spells of three or four minutes each.

Sometimes, for demonstration purposes, we can and do take a wild horse from the mountain and have him riding quite quietly within half an hour or an hour, simply by using signs and sounds the horse understands. But of course normally e.s.p. and telepathy are used on a horse that has been handled and is quite tame, and it is merely a question of getting in tune with him straight away and getting him to do what you want him to do. In getting a horse to do what you want him to do by our methods, you do not have to train him to answer any set words of command: there is no reason at all why he should know the words 'walk on' or 'trot'.

There is a story of a poacher who was stopped by the local policeman and accused of using his dog for poaching. He told the constable that his dog would not hunt rabbits, to which he got a rude answer, so he said 'well I will show you.' So he took the dog and the policeman into a field where there were plenty of rabbits, and said 'go on boy, catch one.' The dog stood where he was. The more he said 'go on and catch one' the more the dog stood where he was, so the policeman gave up in disgust, and went away. As soon as he had gone out of sight, the poacher turned to his dog and said 'get to heel,' and the dog straight away shot out and caught a rabbit. Human words of command, in short, mean nothing to an animal in themselves, and have to be taught. But if you use signs, sounds and signals that the horse understands then you will get a natural response, and it makes the training of your horse infinitely easier.

12: *Making the Most of Your Horse*

There are only three things necessary if you are to learn to comprehend what your horse is trying to say, and make him comprehend what you want him to do: patience, understanding and unlimited time. You will need patience to spend endless hours watching and memorizing the signs and sounds he uses in communicating with you and with other horses; understanding to appreciate that a horse does not think or respond as a human being does; and unlimited time to complete your task, because a task it is, one that has taken us twenty years to complete. Understanding is the most important requirement to begin with. If you look upon your horse as another human being, you will never be able to understand him and make yourself clearly understood by him. You have only to watch a bunch of wild horses in the field together to see that their reactions and behaviour are completely alien to those of the human being. You may see one horse approach another and the first horse turn on him and attack him with his teeth and feet. But you would make a mistake if you concluded that they were enemies. Horses, no matter how friendly, will often kick and bite each other, as human beings will argue with each other, but it is always an instantaneous reaction and it is over in a minute or two. A horse is not human and the greatest barrier to the understanding of any animal is anthropomorphism, that is to say, attributing human personality and behaviour to animals.

It must also be remembered that no animal will react to exactly the same stimuli as another animal. Bearing this in mind, if you wish to understand what your horse is saying, it is probably best to begin by trying to make some semblance of order out of the signs and sounds he uses that you understand already – you will be surprised at how many signs and sounds you do know. If you are in close contact with a large number of horses, it is best to begin by concentrating on one horse, the horse that you feel closest to. When you have discovered how much you already understand of what he is saying, you will be able to start adding to the list. You will find it a very slow process, but after six months, if you have really put your mind to the subject, you should be able to understand most of what he says. You should have between twenty-five and thirty basic messages.

You can now start trying to understand signs and sounds used by other horses you are in contact with, and to find out how they convey the same basic message. For example, if you are in contact with twenty horses, and you take a basic message such as 'welcome', you will probably find eight to a dozen different variations in the way that it is said, so you will add the variations to your vocabulary.

When you have your list of basic messages (forty-seven in all), you can start extending your vocabulary when speaking to the horse. You will of course use your voice, but it does not matter what words you use since it is the tone of the voice that matters to the animal. Alex Kerr, Bertram Mills' lion tamer, used to describe how when he was training a lion or a tiger, he had to work the animal for a very long time indeed, and to get one animal to perform one action might take five or six hours. The whole time he would be talking to the animal he was training, and he found the only way he could relieve his own tension was to swear. So he learnt to swear in as many languages as he could. He would use the foulest oaths under the sun in a soft, caressing, gentle tone – he swore at his lions and tigers to stop himself getting angry with them.

Then when you are using signs, you must remember that your hands and arms cease to be hands and arms, but become neck and head, so that when you stroke the horse it will feel to him that he is being caressed with the head and nose of another horse, and when you slap him it will tingle for him in the same way as a bite from another horse. Other movements you use are very similar to that of a horse: your legs are similar in action to his hind legs, so if for example he kicks at you, it will be exactly the same movement that you use to kick him back.

And if he does kick at you, it is important for you to kick back at him straight away, since if you do not, he will think that he has dominated you by his anger. It is no use whatever if you wait until you come out of hospital, six weeks later. In a herd, you will notice that if an inferior horse kicks at the boss horse, the boss horse will kick back much harder and much more firmly; but if a boss horse kicks at an inferior horse, the inferior horse will get out of the way. So if when your horse kicks at you, you get out of the way, he will immediately assume that you are inferior to him in the social hierarchy of the herd. Only if you attack him back will he accept that you are the boss.

When you can interpret all the signs and sounds that your horses use, and they can interpret what you are saying to them, you can start using your feelings and instincts to interpret his e.s.p. messages. This is not as revolutionary as it sounds. What you are trying to do is to extend an ability that you are using already, for once you can get that feeling of oneness with your horse, it is only a small step to interpreting his moods and feelings.

In the early stages you ought to be able to tell if he is relaxed or excited even before you see him; and the more you handle him, provided that you are thinking on approximately the some wavelength, the more you will understand. The most difficult part of e.s.p., and the danger that has to be guarded against, is the fact that everyone wants to believe he can do it, and that he is indeed getting through to his horse, or whatever animal he is handling. We have found with many people that, while there is a certain amount of e.s.p. response, there is even more imagination. When you really are getting through to a horse, you will know what he is feeling and you will know what he is going to do next, and the certainty of your knowledge will be such that there is no room for doubt whatever – it is impossible to be mistaken. Part of your knowledge is bound to come from using your eyes and ears, and from your knowledge of the horse and the horse's reactions : if a horse puts his ears back and arches his back, you will know that he is going to buck. But when you are getting through to the horse, you will feel the tension increasing and the knots growing in your belly long before there is any visible sign. You will feel his hunger and impatience as you go towards the feeding house, even when you cannot see him and long before he knocks his basin and whickers.

One of the ways to extend your extra-sensory relation with your horse is to ride him without using your reins, guiding him and controlling him entirely with your thoughts. You will find this very difficult at first, but it will improve with time. You should however always remember that you are using a method of communication that leaves the free will of the individual full play. The horse may disagree with you, and if he does, you have no control over him, but can only rely on his good nature. You may say 'let's go left,' and he may say 'no, I am going right.' You may say 'let's trot,' and he may answer by saying 'why should I bother.' But when there is a complete two-way play of e.s.p. and telepathy, you will find this does not occur very often, since you will both want to go the same way.

I have occasional trouble myself with free will. When I let the horses out, I let them free in the yard and they walk down the road or up the hill, directed to the field I want by a mixture of their habit, and my telepathic messages. But sometimes they say 'we are damned if we are going there, we want to go somewhere else,' and when this happens I have to run like the devil to get in front of them. But this sort of conflict is inevitable. When you are controlling a horse with your mind, he must have the freedom to reject your suggestions or accept them at will. The more you are getting through to the horse, the more he will get through to you, and the less often this will occur.

But if you are a weak character, a word of warning in

using my methods. Don't whatever you do allow yourself to become a zombie, your mind and actions controlled by some lazy quadruped, for whom you work sixty hours a week in order to earn enough to keep *him* in the comfort to which he has become accustomed!

Appendix: Some Practical Advice to Horse-owners

The most serious difficulties that arise between horse and owner are those that stem from the plain fact that the two are simply not suited to each other. Either the temperament of the horse is wrong for the owner, or the horse is unsuitable for the purpose for which it is required: for example a nervous person should not have a horse that is any way excitable, and a person who really wants to go should never have a horse that wants only to stand around looking at the horizon.

This is why the purchase of a horse is so important and deserves a deal more thought and preparation than it normally receives.

First of all, where should you buy it? In certain areas horses are much cheaper than in others: broadly speaking, in the belt stretching from London to the Midlands, horses are dearer than they are in other parts of the country. Obviously they are going to be cheaper in those areas which produce horses – the West of England, Wales, Yorkshire and parts of Scotland – and it is much better to go to one of these areas to select the horse to suit you, rather than to some plush dealer's yard in the suburbs. In either case you will probably end up with a very similar horse, the difference being that since the dealer had taken the trouble to go to the West Country or Wales or Ireland to buy that horse and take it back to his yard, you will have to pay fifty to one hundred pounds more than he paid for it. There are of course advantages in buying from a reputable dealer since (a) he is almost certainly a first-class judge of a horse and (b) if the horse you buy is unsuitable he will probably change it for another one. But you will have to pay him very handsomely for his expertise.

On the other hand I would not advise an inexperienced buyer to buy from a private individual, since in my experience private individuals have a grossly inflated idea of their horse's value, and tend to be totally blind to his faults. If you have a very long purse you can buy privately a well-known and well proven horse; but very few of us have long purses and we have to buy the horse we want for as little as possible, which brings us to the place where I buy most of mine, which is at public auction.

To buy a horse at public auction, however, you need to be a reasonable judge of a horse yourself, or to have the advice of someone who is a reasonable judge. The best adviser without any doubt at all is a veterinary surgeon, but since it is extremely difficult to get a veterinary surgeon to come with you to an auction sale, a riding school proprietor who keeps the type of horse you have in mind is a good person to take along – provided of course he has not got a horse he wants to sell you himself! If you are going to an auction, it is important to go to one of the auctions in the horse-producing areas. The ones I know best, being a West-Country man and living in Wales, are Exeter, Abergavenny, Llanybyther (which is my own auction), Hay-on-Wye, Hereford, and Stow-on-the-Wold. At an auction in a horse-producing area a high proportion of the horses are being sold by people who breed horses commercially for sale, on their farms; whereas at the urban auctions you get a large number of throwouts from other people's stables, and so a much higher proportion of unsound horses than at the rural auction.

But of course the rural auctions are usually held in distant places, so you do have the problem and cost of transporting the horses to your home. There are three ways this can be done. You can go to the auction and contact someone there who expects to have an empty lorry going home. This is a little bit chancy. Or you can hire a Land-Rover and trailer yourself; or, ideally, persuade someone else to go down with you to buy a horse, and bring yours back in his Land-Rover and trailer. This will give you the additional advantage of an adviser on tap!

The type of horse to aim to buy at an auction is in fact something looking a little bit rough and thin, since this horse will increase in value. If you buy a horse already looking smart and polished it will cost you a lot more money, and at the same time there is always a chance that the spit and polish has been put there to hide some of his more glaring faults.

It is worth remembering, too, when you buy at a public auction, that you have four days to test out any warranty on that horse, and it is most important that you do this. If you buy a horse that is warranted as sound, as soon as you get it home you must have it thoroughly vetted. If you get a horse that is said to be quiet to ride in traffic, ride him in heavy traffic at once. It is also advisable to understand the various claims made about the horse in a catalogue. If it says that the horse is quiet to ride, it means in law just that. If it says he is a good jumper, check that he is a good jumper. If it says he is suitable for a beginner, find the biggest beginner you know and put him on the horse and see how he gets on. Mind you, I have my own interpretations of the sales catalogue descriptions. They go something like this: 'quiet to ride' means, roughly, 'has not bucked or bolted with anyone for a week and the vendor hopes it will not buck you off before the four days run out'. 'Recently broken' means that the vendor was hoping to sell it as a quiet ride, but the horse bucked his son off the day before yesterday and so he cannot give him that warranty. 'Has been backed' means the owner's son was put on and bucked off immediately. 'Will make a one-day-eventer' means that he will not make a show-jumper, point-to-pointer or a dressage horse. 'Good hunter' means 'will go out hunting provided you do not go too near the hounds and do not leave the road'. But this is just my rather humorous way of expressing a necessary scepticism. Never, never, never believe anything anybody tells you about a horse he is trying to sell. He probably believes it himself, but horse owners are rather like mothers, they cannot see any faults in their children, though they can see all their virtues. When you are buying a horse it is the faults you want to know about, not the virtues.

But do not let the foregoing discourage you. Provided you go to a rural auction, you should get a horse much cheaper than you will get it anywhere else, and you have the chance of buying a very good horse that has not done very much work. Always remember that ponies up to about fourteen-two are much cheaper in autumn than in the spring, and that hunters are much cheaper in the spring than in the autumn.

The type of horse you buy is of course of vital importance. First of all think honestly about your own personality. If you are in any way nervous or if you are worried about riding in heavy traffic you must get a quiet horse. It is no good buying a thoroughbred or an Arab because they tend to be excitable. If on the other hand you are a keen person and want to go in for competition work this type of horse is extremely suitable. If the horse has to be out all winter you must get one of the mountain or moorland types, since they winter out very well, whilst the thoroughbreds and Arabs need to be in. Again, one of the advantages of buying at an auction sale is that you will have a large number of horses to choose from, while even at the biggest dealer's yards there will be only a few of the type you want.

When you are at the auction buying the horse, the key to his personality can very often be seen in his behaviour as he stands in the stable, and as he stands outside the ring walking in and out amongst the crowd. The crowd will worry some horses, but it will not worry others. Some will be irritable and some will be placid. This will tell you something. But above all, the important thing is to pick the horse that you click with mentally: the horse that seems to be talking to you and not to anybody else. Buying a horse, I often think, is far more important than picking a wife. After all when you pick a wife it is only going to cost you a seven-and-sixpence licence, and if you are a little bit careful about your choice you can make her go out to work and keep you in the manner to which you would like to become accustomed. But if you are picking a horse it is going to cost you a hell of a lot of money in the first place and on top of this it is going to cost you six or seven pounds a week to keep it, which makes it a very different proposition. If you have got the right horse it is worth while, if you have got the wrong horse it is hell.

You have now bought your horse, for better or for worse, and you have managed to get it home and all the local horse pundits have been round to look at it and said nice things about it to your face and nasty things about it behind your back. This is absolutely inevitable, it does not matter what horse you buy they will always criticize it behind your back. But having got that over, and having tried it out thoroughly to see that its warranty is true, it is time to start working on him. If he is out, it is vital, to begin with anyway, that you see and handle and talk to him every day. This means quite simply whether you are riding him or not, that you must go out and spend half-an-hour to an hour talking to him in a field. And it is no good standing at the top of the field and carrying on a shouted conversation with him down at the far end. You want to fill your pockets with horse- and pony-nuts and go down and feed him one or two at a time, talk to him and watch him and thoroughly get to know him. Get to know him as a person. You will know you are beginning to get through to him when he does two things: first, when he gives you a whicker of welcome and comes over to talk to you; and second, when you see him start driving any other horses in the field away when they try to come to talk to you. This last will show you that you have become his, you belong to him, and he will look after you and do anything for you.

The next thing you will have to do is to catch your horse, and strangely enough I have found that there is a greater ignorance about catching horses than about anything else to do with them. Why this is I do not quite know – probably because most horses are extremely easy to catch – but if you have a horse that is in any way difficult, there is a standard procedure for catching him. First of all you have to get him to come to the bucket, and when he comes to eat out of a bucket quite happily and quietly, you can set about teaching him to be caught. You very slowly get him eating out of the bucket until he walks past you. Most horses, no matter how difficult, will come and pick out of a bucket at arm's length. Once they have really started eating you bring the bucket closer to you and then you bring it past you, until you are standing by the shoulder of the horse. Then you can slip your arm over the neck and make a fuss of him. Having done this you put the halter rope round his neck. If he tries to break away, let him go. Do not hang on, this is the worst thing you can do. He is much stronger than you and the chances are three to one that he will get away anyway. All you do is let him go and start again. Again you lead him past your body, put your arm over his neck, and slip the rope over his neck. Having done that you put the halter on from the far side, *not* the near side. If you try to put the halter on from the near side, he will swing away from the halter and away from you and get away. But if you put the halter on the far side of his head, the side away from you, if he swings away from the halter, he swings towards you, which means that if you go on quietly you can slip the halter on quite easily. Again, if you have a difficult horse to catch, it is usually far simpler to lead him into the stable following a bucket (provided the stable is reasonably near the field and there are no busy main roads to cross), than it is to halter him in the field and lead him in with the halter.

I had to use this technique only a short time ago. Four of our horses got out on to Llanybyther mountain, and it so happened that two of them were young horses who had never been haltered and the other two were very difficult to catch anyway. But I had been feeding them in the field, and when I went up to talk to them they would come up and eat out of the bucket. After about two hours looking, we managed to find them about three miles away across the mountain. So, I just stood there, about three or four hundred yards away from them, rattled the bucket and shouted, and they came hell for leather. As soon as they each had a mouthful out of the bucket, I started to walk home, and all four of them followed me the three miles home, taking a mouthful every now and then, without any trouble at all. If I had tried to catch and halter those horses, I would have spent hours at it. Possibly it would have been better if I had spent the time teaching them to be caught, but two thousand acres of open mountain is not an ideal situation for teaching a horse to be caught. That is something you want to do in a reasonably confined space, in our experience a yard about twenty yards by thirty yards.

You will of course at times have your horse in the stable. He may be in the stable all the time or you may just bring him in to saddle and bridle him. But it is here that the really important work is done. You must get your horse understanding you, get him to understand what you want him to do quite clearly, and at the same time you must be consistent. It is no good teaching him one day to eat out of your pocket and the next day hitting him on the nose for doing just that. It is here that you teach him that he is a subordinate member of the herd to you, and that you are boss. You must not let him push you about, and if he bites or kicks you, bite or kick him back. There are no two ways about this. Just as he must trust you in every way, you must be able to trust him absolutely, and you have no hope whatsoever of being able to control him riding, if you cannot control him on the ground. If you are afraid of him on the ground you will be afraid of him on his back, and it is on the ground and in the stable that you develop trust with your horse. If you are unable to do this it is far better to sell him at once to someone who can handle him, rather than keep him yourself. This is perhaps not important as far as you are concerned, but what does concern me is that your horse will not be happy.

It is a piece of supreme arrogance to think that you will look after your horse better than anyone else and that you will love him more than anyone else will. Most people love their horses or they would not keep them, and most people look after them to the best of their ability, so it is important for the horse that he should be owned by someone who can handle and understand him, rather than be owned by someone who is a little bit afraid of him. A spoilt horse is rather like a spoilt child : he is unhappy, discontented and he tends to be ill-treated. Today in my opinion there is far more ill-treatment of horses and dogs through over-indulgence and lack of discipline than there is through outright cruelty.

The whole time you are in the field with the horse and in the stable with the horse, as well as when you are riding him, you should be talking to him and trying to observe and understand the signs and sounds he uses to you. This will lead to a better understanding between you and the horse and to a much better performance.

Feeding is quite simple. A horse should be well fed but not over-fed. There has been a great deal written in countless books about feeding, so I am not going into it in detail here, but the most important thing to remember about grazing is that the horse is a selective feeder and a field that to the layman's eye may have an awful lot of grass in it, may be starvation conditions for a horse, as a horse likes short sweet grass and will not eat tough grass. Long rank grass is not suitable grazing for a horse or a pony.

I have dealt with discipline on the ground, and discipline when you are riding is very similar. We aim to have all our horses enjoying what they are doing as much as possible, but there are times when the horse has to do things that he does not enjoy doing. But it does not matter what we ask a horse to do, he must do just that. I always say that if I asked a horse to climb Mount Everest the horse would have to climb Mount Everest, but of course you must never ask a horse to do something he is not capable of doing. If you have asked him to do something, you must persevere until he does it.

Before now I have spent four hours trying to get a horse to walk over a low bank when there was an open gateway twenty yards further down. I had turned him over the low bank before I got to the gate because it seemed quicker, to save myself half a minute; but the horse said he would not go over, so I just stayed there, and kept walking him into the bank until he walked over and it took me four hours to do it. First I asked Winberto to walk over the bank, and Winberto said 'no', so having said 'please will you walk over the bank' and had the reply 'no I will not', I then insisted 'you have damned well got to.' When we are handling our horses we always say 'please will you'', but at the back of that 'please' is the determination that the horse will have to do it anyway. You do the basic work on this on the ground, if you walk into him when he is standing in your way, you ask him 'please will you get out of my way,' and if he still stands there you catch him a slap so that he knows he must get out of the way because you are boss. But you can only do this with a horse when you know and understand him, so that when you smack him, he will stand back and say 'what the hell was that for?' And two minutes later he is all over you again. We always say that when you have a row with a horse you have to make it up with him afterwards. After having had a fight with a difficult horse we go and make a terrific fuss of him. I would not like you to think that I spend a lot of my time hitting my horses, because I do not, I very rarely hit or clout a horse and when I am riding it is the exception when I carry a stick with me. But there is no point in my giving advice on how to deal with a horse who behaves perfectly, so I have picked on the exceptional cases when discipline is necessary. I always say I only have to hit a horse once if he is being a little bit difficult. I pick a situation where he is going to say 'no I will not,' and then I hit him hard and when I hit a horse I hit him hard. I do not tap, tap with a stick, I really lace him on both sides so that afterwards he will always remember being hit and I do not have to hit him again. There is nothing that annoys me more, when I

am watching people riding, than to see them tap, tap, tap
with the stick. It is not doing the horse any good, it only
annoys him. It is far better if you are going to use a stick to
really use it. But of course you must never on any occasion
hit a horse unless he is doing something that is very wrong.

You should be able to get the maximum amount of
scolding into your voice. I always aim to be able, when I have
had a horse for about three weeks, to go into a field and shout
'come on my darlings' and have all the horses come galloping over to me. When I am handling or riding a horse, after
two or three months a horse should do anything I want
him to, without my actually asking him. I like my horses to
anticipate what I want. As soon as I show a horse a jump, he
should be tearing to get over it. When you take your horse out
for a ride, it is important that you are enjoying what you are
going to do, but it is equally important that your horse should
enjoy it, since if both your horse and you are enjoying what
you are doing you will add to each other's enjoyment. I hate
watching the German riders on television, because they tend
towards a type of precision and discipline that treats the horse
as a robot and not as another person. The rider dominates
and demands obedience. Even for a horse that is handled
only at week-ends a certain amount of schooling is important,
since it will increase the horse's ability and enjoyment and
so increase your own enjoyment; but the type of schooling
you give him depends on what you want to do. The dressage
type of schooling is very fashionable at the moment, though I
far prefer the polo type. Dressage schooling involves doing
everything on an even stride and all your movements have
to be even and smooth, whereas the polo type of schooling
involves far more abrupt movements and teaches the horse
to work off an uneven stride. It is fine preparation for cross
country work, steeple-chasing and hunting, since in any of
these pursuits you will tend to get situations where you have
to jump on an uneven stride, or turn very sharply, and a
horse that will change legs at a mere shift of your body and
can jump and turn at the same time, and put himself right

and shorten and extend his stride automatically, has a very great advantage. I find dressage work uncongenial also because anticipation is very much discouraged, whereas I like my horses to anticipate what I am going to ask them to do and do it before they have been asked.

But whatever form of schooling you decide upon, it is extremely important that you should never have a fight with your horse during a schooling session. He should look on your schooling area as a place where he is going to enjoy himself, and not associate it with an unpleasant experience. You should start teaching your horse the basic things you want to school him in during a normal ride : for example if you want to teach your horse to back, you should get him backing before you take him into the schooling area, which should be the place where you put polish on to the movements the horse is already doing. When you want to teach your horse to jump, the simple way to do it is when you are out riding normally. You get three or four horses cantering along in front of you, and just pop over a tree trunk lying on the ground – anything small, about one foot to eighteen inches high, just so that the horse has to take off – and you will find that instead of having to teach the horse to jump he will come to jumping quite naturally. It is best if you can find a fence without a lot of daylight on either side of it. With nine horses out of ten, if three or four horses are cantering along in front of him, and he is tearing along to catch up with them, just as they pop over the tree trunk he will jump over quite naturally. After that, whenever you see a small obstacle you can jump, you just pop over it, and slowly by degrees the jumps that you take him over will rise in height.

This comes back to the basic principle of teaching a horse to do anything : if he sees other horses doing it and enjoying it, and you are looking forward to doing it and enjoying it yourself, the horse will also want to do it.

A classic example of this interaction happened to me about twenty years ago. I had a young chestnut thoroughbred which I had just started riding, and I had only been riding him about ten days when the hounds met nearby. I took him out to have a look, mainly to give him an interest and he enjoyed it and found time went quite quickly. I was with a friend of mine, Bill Manfield, and we cantered down the lane and came round the corner and there was a three-foot-six-inch gate right across the lane. Bill was on his very good hunter, Melody, and he as a matter of course went straight on over it and before I knew anything the three-year-old had followed the mare. He had never jumped anything in his life, and the first thing he jumped was a three-foot-six-inch gate. This just shows what can be done, provided you take something as it arises in its natural course, and do not make a great issue of doing anything. If you treat the young horse as if he had been doing it all his life, he will do it, but if you go into it wondering 'will he or won't he, can he or can't he,' the horse is sure to stop. If you enjoy jumping your horse will enjoy jumping and will jump well. If you do not like jumping, your horse will not, and if neither of you likes jumping, do not jump. This is the key to the whole thing.

Finally, here are some do's and don'ts when you are handling your horse. Do get a horse that suits your temperament, do not get one that is beyond your abilities. Do remember that beauty is only skin deep and do not be taken in by spit and polish. Do remember that a horse who looks rough and thin can always be improved, whereas one who is fat, glossy and finished can only lose in value. Do be boss and do not be dominated by your horse. Do what you enjoy doing, do not do something just because your friends do it. Do observe his signs and sounds, but do not let your imagination run away with you. Back everything up with sound observations. Do say 'please will you' before you ask a horse to do anything, and be sure to back it up with determination to enforce your wishes. But above all do not ask a horse to perform beyond his capabilities. Do school regularly but do not fight in the schooling arena. Do think like a horse but do not endow him with human qualities, feelings and responses, because he is not a human being – fortunately for the horse! Do observe his natural wishes and desires, but do not spoil him. Do enforce discipline but do not be a martinet. Do teach him to jump naturally, but do not over-jump him : about twelve to fifteen fences a day is enough for most horses. Last of all please remember that it is important for the horse to enjoy himself, to be happy and to be comfortable, but that this cannot be achieved without firmness and discipline.